Project Politics

Project Politics

A Systematic Approach to Managing Complex Relationships

NITA A. MARTIN
Pure Indigo, UK

Routledge
Taylor & Francis Group

LONDON AND NEW YORK

First published in paperback 2024

First published 2011 by Gower Publishing

Published 2016 by Routledge
4 Park Square, Milton Park, Abingdon, Oxon OX14 4RN

and by Routledge
605 Third Avenue, New York, NY 10158

Routledge is an imprint of the Taylor & Francis Group, an informa business

© 2011, 2016, 2024 Nita A. Martin

The right of Nita A. Martin to be identified as author of this work has been asserted in accordance with sections 77 and 78 of the Copyright, Designs and Patents Act 1988.

Publisher's Note
The publisher has gone to great lengths to ensure the quality of this reprint but points out that some imperfections in the original copies may be apparent.

This publication is designed to provide information regarding the subject matter covered. Neither the author nor the publishers are engaged in rendering legal, accounting or other professional service through this publication. If legal advice or other expert assistance is required, the services of an appropriate professional person should be sought. Whilst every effort has been made to ensure that the content of this book is accurate, neither the author nor the publishers can accept responsibility for any loss sustained as a result of the use of this material.

British Library Cataloguing in Publication Data
Martin, Nita A.
    Project politics : a systematic approach to managing complex relationships.
    1. Project management. 2. Teams in the workplace – Management. 3. Psychology, Industrial.
    I. Title
    658.4'04–dc22

Library of Congress Cataloging-in-Publication Data
Martin, Nita A.
    Project politics : a systematic approach to managing complex relationships / by Nita A. Martin.
    p. cm.
    Includes index.
    ISBN 978-0-566-08895-7(hbk)
  1. Project management. 2. Interpersonal relations. I. Title.

    HD69.P75M375 2010
    658.4'04–dc22

2010024943

ISBN: 978-0-566-08895-7 (hbk)
ISBN: 978-1-03-283823-6 (pbk)
ISBN: 978-1-315-60243-1 (ebk)

DOI: 10.4324/9781315602431

Contents

List of Tables

Introduction

About Project Politics

Politics is defined as the process by which decisions are made by people. It is the essence of governing and it includes both the administration and control of internal and external affairs. The term 'politics' is often used in a project environment, where it also refers to the way in which projects are governed. On projects, both the formal and informal processes and the situations which arise are considered part of the politics. Projects, by their very nature, are often unique activities. This can make that environment stressful, since there may be little to benchmark accurately against from either personal experience or from best practice and research. Thus politics can have a significant effect in these situations.

The ability of individuals to work together and manage relationships to facilitate the delivery of a project can be a major factor in determining project success. Some people are aware of workplace politics, and others are not. Some get emotionally affected and others are able to remain detached. Some are excellent at taking advantage of political situations through careful manipulation and others just seem to be victims of the events that unfold around them. Each individual's awareness and how they are affected by politics can differ and often be unpredictable. It is easy to assume that others will react in the same way as us and so we are surprised when they do not.

Even a project manager who has mastered all the tools of the trade may still struggle to deliver projects successfully due to misinterpreting or even missing the signs of underlying political issues. Politics and the personalities of those involved can be a greater influence in making a project successful than the project management skill base of the team. In fact, even the lightest touch of project management disciplines can result in resounding success, if people work together and there are no hidden agendas at play, for example:

- Developing one's career,

- Improving visibility in the organization,

- Making a lasting contribution, and

- Disassociating from projects that have a chance of failure.

Regardless of the product or service provided, it is unimaginable to see any business successfully distance itself from the issues that arise from human interaction. Regardless of whether you are a project manager, a project team member or the end user or customer of the project's deliverables, understanding that politics can play a big part in the way that projects pan out should lead to reduced anxiety and frustration on projects.

This book focuses on political situations that arise in project environments. The following professionals may come across the type of case studies discussed in this book.

- Project managers,

- Project teams,

- Performance managers,

- Risk managers,

- Internal audit teams,

- Due diligence teams,

- Managers of small and medium businesses, and

- Senior managers of large businesses.

The key is to remember that it is not only your particular project that suffers from politics. You will need to take politics in your stride and, in order to be successful, find ways to achieve what you want in such environments.

A Systematic Approach

Project Politics provides a framework for problem solving political issues. The structured approach presented can raise your awareness and improve your ability to manage issues in the work place. It aims to provide a structure to identify what actions could be taken. Even if you do not wish to influence the situation, you may find some comfort in understanding the politics better. Once you recognize the issues, you can then generate pragmatic solutions to deal with them.

DEALING WITH POLITICAL SITUATIONS

1.   Reflect on your motivations, your ways of working and your ability to influence others.
2.   Reflect on others' motivations, their ways of working and their ability to influence others.
3.   Look out for political situations as they arise.
4.   Use the concepts presented in this book to structure your problem solving and generate potential solutions.

Structure of this Book

PART I – MODELLING HUMAN BEHAVIOUR

This book is split into two parts. In Part I, some theoretical concepts of human behaviour are presented. These models consider aspects such as psychology, influence, behaviour and communication. They form a starting point for structuring your observations and understanding why people behave the way they do. The concepts presented in this book are reasonably well known. Some, for example, are used for assessing people during job interviews and training sessions. The objective is to encourage the use of knowledge that you may already have. This can then form the basis of further research in this area to support the development of your political problem solving abilities. The chapters in this section of the book are as follows: Chapter 1 'Psychological Profiling Models', Chapter 2 'Influence Models', Chapter 3 'Behaviour Models', Chapter 4 'Communication Models'.

PART II – CASE STUDIES BY PROJECT LIFESTYLE STAGE

The second part of this book is structured using the familiar project life cycle. Each project stage is considered in turn and case studies are presented with analyses that draw upon the concepts in Part I. The chapters in this section of the book are as follows: Chapter 5 'Project Definition', Chapter 6 'Planning and Risk Management', Chapter 7 'Implementation', Chapter 8 'Project Evaluation and Closure'.

PART I
Modelling Human Behaviour

Introduction

When you are in the heat of project delivery and wrestling with deadlines, it can be difficult to take a step back and look at the situation objectively. You may find it even more difficult to think about how any theoretical models that you may be familiar with could be useful. These models and concepts can help rationalize situations, even without detailed application. They can be used to structure your thoughts and identify ways to proceed, creating options in even very difficult situations. You can often usefully apply the fundamentals of these models without performing a detailed analytical investigation. It is not always possible to talk through political situations with colleagues or to receive support from friends and family. This is where even a light touch but structured approach using academic models can help provide a solution.

This chapter looks at some established models and concepts that can be utilized to understand charged political project environments. The aim is not to overwhelm you with academic research and constraints, but to enable you to draw upon some of the outcomes to form solutions and draw conclusions relevant to your own situation. These models are often used for personality profiling and training and development programmes. You may even have come across them at job interviews or at team building events.

Remember that these concepts are approximations of otherwise complex human behaviours. They should not be used to classify individuals. People can change and just because they behaved in one way today does not mean that they will behave in exactly the same way tomorrow. You need to be pragmatic in your use of such theories, in the same way that you need to be pragmatic in the application of project management techniques.

The table below summarizes the models presented in Part I of this book. They have been categorized into psychological, influential, behavioural and communication models. A simplified overview only is provided for each of the models. The objective is to focus on the fundamental structures that they provide rather than the method of performing detailed analyses.

Table I.1   Models and concepts of human behaviour

Type	Description
Psychological profiling	Maslow's theory of human motivation. Myers-Brigg type indicator (MBTI).
Influence	Types of influence. Degrees of influence. Methods of influence.
Behavioural	Belbin team inventory. Organizational anti-patterns. Tactics.
Communication	Neuro-linguistic programming (NLP). Transactional analysis (TA).

Psychological Profiling Models

Two well-known psychological models are described. The first is Maslow's theory of motivation and the second is Myers-Briggs type indicator. Maslow's theory is useful because it models motivation and how it can change depending on the circumstances. Maslow describes a five-layer model and explains that we are driven by fundamental needs from either one or more of the layers. As soon as some of these needs are met, then the desire to fulfil new needs arises, leading to a constant feeling of dissatisfaction. This hierarchy of motivation can be used to determine the underlying reasons for political issues.

Myers-Briggs type indicator – a model that describes psychological types that people are born with or that they develop – can be utilized for differentiating between personality types. This information can be used for directing effective management and engagement.

Maslow's Theory of Human Motivation

This is a popular theory on human motivation. Maslow described five levels of needs, where each level represented a need that must first be acquired and maintained before moving on to the next level (Maslow, 1943). In this way, as soon as the requirements of one stage were fulfilled, a new desire emerged to replace it. This continual emergence of a new desire is what leaves a person always feeling unsatisfied (at least to some degree). It is therefore the nature of humans always to desire more. For further information see Maslow (1998) and King (2009).

Maslow's hierarchy can be a particularly useful model in understanding motivations and why they differ from person to person. For example, some individuals are always keen to get the next promotion and to take on more responsibility. On the other hand, some individuals simply want to keep their head down and get on with their work. They have no desire to be promoted, to manage more people or take on additional responsibility. Maslow's framework can provide a structure for grading individuals and understanding their motivations. The five levels of the hierarchy are described below.

Table 1.1   Maslow's hierarchy of needs

Level 1	Physiological
Level 2	Safety
Level 3	Love and belonging
Level 4	Self esteem
Level 5	Self actualization

LEVEL 1– PHYSIOLOGICAL

The most fundamental need described by Maslow is that for food, water and sleep. Once these basic physiological requirements of nutrition and rest are met, then a desire for safety can emerge.

In the workplace, level one needs can be interpreted, for example, as a desire for cash flow, thus ensuring sufficient funds to maintain a certain standard of living. It is possible to ignore or compromise physiological needs in the workplace. Take the example of making people work late coming up to a deadline. Installing a culture of sleep deprivation and hunger will demotivate individuals as their most fundamental physiological needs will not have been met.

LEVEL 2 – SAFETY

Once physiological needs have been met, they are often forgotten or taken for granted since they are no longer threatened. At this stage, a new desire emerges; a desire for security and safety. This need is often met by living in a healthy society, where there are, for example, no threats from the wild and crime rates are low (in particular, violent crime). This is a need that society as a whole can provide, enabling the individual to focus on the next, higher, stages of human motivation.

There are less extreme examples of the search for safety and security however. We tend to feel safe when situations are predictable, familiar and routine, for example:

- Controlling change or even reducing it,

- Adopting risk averse behaviour,

- Seeking to understand the world through science, religion and philosophy, and

- Compulsive–obsessive disorder reducing anxiety through repeated behaviours.

Some examples of risk reduction techniques include:

- Buying insurance to deal with the unexpected,

- Preferring job security over job prospects,

- Saving and investing in pensions rather than spending, and

- Purchasing branded equipment with guarantees.

Implementing a project, by its very nature, involves doing something new or making a change. Change management is an essential part of making people feel secure and it is rarely implemented well. A simple example is that of mass redundancies during an economic downturn. Even though the redundancy process needs to be handled carefully, even the largest of organizations employing change and communication managers can fail to professionally manage this process.

LEVEL 3 – LOVE AND BELONGING

Once the need for safety is sufficiently satisfied, the desire to be loved and to belong to a group emerges; seeking acceptance, affection and validation from family, friends and colleagues. Examples include:

- Being in a loving relationship,

- Having good relationships with family,

- Joining clubs and societies or taking part in social group activities,

- Working with other people and feeling valued, and

- Being an active part of a community.

In the workplace, this need can be met through being part of a team or from being gainfully employed. This need can also manifest itself negatively. For example, reluctantly accepting the consensus or acting under peer pressure. Behavioural traits such as these are discussed further in Chapter 3.

LEVEL 4 – SELF ESTEEM

Next, the desire for improving self esteem and self respect is considered. This also includes the need to be respected by others. Employment is a process through which self esteem is often improved. Being a valued member of an organization and contributing to its success, with your skills and talents being in demand, can be a key factor in establishing self esteem. Other examples include:

- Being in a relationship where you feel valued,

- Having a family that values your contribution,

- Feeling that your presence in the world makes a difference, and

- Receiving acknowledgement for your efforts at work or in clubs and societies.

The need for self esteem in a business environment can be seen in the way that individual team members want to be valued and have their efforts recognized. They want to feel that the tasks that they are doing make a difference. This desire can often be one that is difficult to manage. As a project manager, you may have to set multiple tasks to people. If of the ten tasks that were meant to be completed, only four are, what can you do to get the others done? You cannot make anyone do them. So you have to find diplomatic ways to achieve the required result. Making it clear that a task's outcome is valuable and that there will be clear recognition and praise for its completion is a positive way in which you can approach this. Tasks which are considered mundane can often be the ones that people need the greatest motivation for. Understanding that contributions need to be openly valued can help you manage these situations better. Ensuring staff understand the need for a given task, no matter how mundane, should help motivate them to complete it.

LEVEL 5 – SELF ACTUALIZATION

Once the need for self esteem is fulfilled, then a desire for self actualization may emerge. This can manifest itself as a desire to fulfil your potential. In artists, this need can be met through the process of creation, such as painting and writing. In this state, you are beginning to achieve your dreams. This level is summarized below:

- Fulfilling your potential,

- Creating something,

- Seeing your dreams become reality, and

- Achieving your ideal role or state.

Most do not achieve level five. Indeed, Maslow stated that even those who reach level four are rare. The need for self actualization can also show up on a project. It can cause issues during project staffing and engagement. It may be that the most reliable and star performers are the ones who need to feel that they are fulfilling their potential. This can lead to them wanting to be involved in projects that allow them to be creative, achieve their ambitions and stretch them through challenge and further development. For this reason, these individuals may need to be moved on to new a new role even if they are doing a great job where they are. Keeping them motivated and excited about coming into work can be a challenge.

APPLICATION

Remember that everyone can experience different levels of need within the hierarchy at different times. Needs are situational; during a recession, when unemployment is high and confidence is low, many experience a return to ensuring that the most basic needs are met. If you lose your job, it could mean that you run the risk of not being able to meet mortgage repayments, or to support your family. Certain types of crime may also increase during recessions and this can impact feelings of security.

This level-based assessment of human motivation can also be used in a more positive way, rather than simply to understand potentially negative behaviours on a project. You can use it to assess how best to motivate your team; more money is nice, but it isn't always enough. They may need to:

- Become a genuine part of the team by taking part in decision making,

- Feel that their contribution has a meaningful impact,

- Work in a challenging environment, and

- Have their needs and those of the project understood and valued.

Motivation is personal. What motivates one person may not work with another and what motivates somebody on one day may not have the same effect in different circumstances. Having a one-size-fits-all strategy for motivation is unlikely to work. In the workplace, generally speaking, the first three levels are maintained by being in work. The next two levels are where it may be possible to apply the most influence. Each level may not be completely satisfied; in general, however, you would expect to see a decreasing level of satisfaction for the higher level categories because they are more difficult to attain.

Myers-Briggs Type Indicator (MBTI)

This model is often used as part of the interviewing process or in team building programmes (Myers and Myers, 1995). It was based on work done by Jung on psychological types. Jung classified two equal pairs of cognitive functions (Jung, 1992).

- Decision making rational functions: Thinking and Feeling, and

- Information gathering irrational functions: Sensing and Intuition.

Jung believed that these functions were expressed either in an Introvert or Extrovert form. Myers-Briggs (Myers and Myers, 1995) added to this theory by presenting personality types and believed that people had an inherent way of thinking and acting that could be classified through their model. The categories that they use for classification are described below.

The Myers-Briggs personality type model considers individuals as being either born with or developing certain preferred ways of thinking and acting. The MBTI model proposes four opposite pairs with a resulting 16 possible combinations of psychological types. These opposing pairs are shown in the table below.

Table 1.2   Myers-Briggs personality type opposing pairs

Functions	Opposing pairs	
Attitude	(E) Extroversion	(I) Introversion
Information gathering	(S) Sensing	(N) Intuition
Decision making	(T) Thinking	(F) Feeling
Lifestyle	(J) Judging	(P) Perceiving

None of these types is intrinsically good or bad. People have a natural tendency towards some of the personality types more than others. The MBTI model can also identify a person's opposite personality type. People tend to find using their opposite psychological preferences more difficult, even if they become more proficient with practice. Myers-Briggs built on Jung's theory by adding the Judging and Perceiving classifications, based on an individual's preference for the decision making or information gathering functions.

The four-letter classification of the sixteen psychological types, for example, ENTJ, is then interpreted not just as the four parts on their own but in a way that takes into account how each part interacts with the other three (Kroeger and Thuesen, 1989; Kummerow, 2004). The table below describes each of the eight characteristics. Of the four functions, Myers-Briggs believed that one would be dominant. The least dominant or inferior function was always considered to be the one that was the opposite of the dominant one. Each of these functions could be used in an extroverted or introverted way.

These eight characteristics shown in the table have specific meanings in the context of Myers-Briggs. It is the direction of the preference that is considered to be more important rather than the extent to which each person displays the characteristic. That is not to say that each person only displays one side of the behaviour, but rather that they have a natural preference for one, although they are able to train themselves perhaps to behave in a different way to their natural instinct. Note that:

1.   The sensing/intuition functions are how new information is understood and interpreted.

2.   The thinking/feeling functions are how decisions are made based on the information gathered using the sensing/intuition function.

3.   For extroverts, the judging/perceiving functions indicate their dominant function and for introverts it is actually auxiliary.

Table 1.3   The eight classifications in the Myers-Briggs type indicator model

Extroversion	Introversion
Prefer to act and then to reflect and then act again. Lose motivation and momentum through inaction. Prefer breadth of thought and to engage with people. Prefer frequent and brief interaction.	Prefer to reflect and then to act and then to reflect further. Recharge ready for action during time of reflection. Prefer depth of thought and to search for ideas and concepts internally. Prefer infrequent but depth of interaction.
Sensing	**Intuition**
Prefer hard information like data and facts.	Trust information that is more abstract, like theories, memories and insight.
Thinking	**Feeling**
Decision making through reasonable, logical, and consistent methods. Will be more concerned with hard project objectives.	Decision making through empathy, diplomacy and the best fit based on weighing up the situation. Will consider the needs of the people involved.
Judging	**Perceiving**
Prefer the decision making function rather than the information gathering function.	Prefer the information gathering function rather than the decision making function.

APPLICATION

This structure can be used to consider the different ways in which people:

•   Prefer to gather information,

•   Prefer to be communicated with, and

•   Make decisions.

Therefore, it can provide information on how to approach people, as some may be more open to hard facts and figures while others will be more receptive to ideas, theories and lessons learned from personal experience and anecdotal information. Accepting that people prefer to work in different ways can make it easier to work effectively with and to manage others.

2

Influence Models

This chapter looks at the types, degrees and methods of influence. Two types of influence can be categorized; namely soft and hard. Soft influence utilizes communication, engagement and knowledge sharing. Hard influence introduces laws, rules, regulations and incentive structures. Knowing that there are different types of influence can lead to the creation of options for approaches that could be tested. Normally combinations of hard and soft influence are used to get the desired results.

A person can be influenced not only in different ways but also to differing extents. For example, Kelman (1958) presented three degrees of possible influence. The first was compliance, regardless of whether agreement had been achieved. The second was the agreement through the changing of attitudes, for example, through the use of an influential figure such as a celebrity or Chief Executive Officer (CEO). The third was both the public and private acceptance of a particular belief (internalization). Knowing that there are different levels to which you can influence can be used to clearly define the required outcome.

Once you have identified the objective of your influencing activity, you then need to have a method of putting that into practice. Exemplary methods include using charisma, reputation, bully pulpit, peer pressure and centres of influence. You are likely to have been exposed to all of these methods. Developing your overall understanding about influence will also aid the recognition of when it is being applied to you. Further information can be found in Owen (2009), Cialdini (2007), Carnegie (2007), Pfeffer (1993) and Cohen and Bradford (2004).

Types of Influence

Influence can be considered as the ability to have power over others. It is a core skill required in business and it is often seen used in the following situations:

- Leadership,

- Motivation and persuasion,

- Business development,

- Sales and marketing,

- Management, and

- Communication and engagement.

The concepts of soft and hard influence (or power) are commonly used in politics. Soft influence is practised through the use of communication and knowledge sharing methods. Hard influence on the other hand is practised through the introduction of rules and incentive structures.

Table 2.1   The two main types of influence

Soft influence	Influence through communication, engagement and knowledge sharing.
Hard influence	Influence through introducing laws, rules, regulations and incentive structures.

APPLICATION

In real world politics, a combination of the two forms of influence is normally used. Realizing that there are two main modes of influence can also be useful during project implementations. Sometimes you can make formal changes to due process, but without the effective use of soft influence these changes may have no effect at all. Successful project management tends also to use both forms of influence. The processes of planning, reporting and assigning tasks provide the formal backbone and then, through effective communication and engagement, delivery is sought.

In the workplace, it is rarely possible to change formal company rules and processes or internal appraisal and performance management systems and so you need to rely more on softer influence. However, if you happen to be the CEO of the company, then it may be easier to create change using hard power; even then you still may not achieve your goal without the use of soft influence. Knowing that there are two types of influence you can develop work plans that make the best use of all of the methods available to you. Additionally, you can ensure that your soft techniques are aligned to and in support of your hard techniques.

Degrees of Influence

Herbert Kelman (1958), a Harvard psychologist, identified three ways in which people can be influenced by others. These three classes of attitude change are described in the table below. You may need to use various methods of influence if you are trying to reach a large group of people, because individuals can respond to each method in different ways.

Table 2.2   The three levels of attitude change

1. Compliance	This is when somebody only appears to accept a belief or behaviour and keeps their actual opinion private.
2. Identification	This is when a person is influenced by someone who is liked and respected, such as a celebrity or a favourite colleague.
3. Internalization	This is when someone accepts a belief or behaviour and agrees both publicly and privately.

APPLICATION

Compliance is a common form of social influence. Often seen in meetings where there is apparent harmony and even resounding agreement, even though people do not agree, they will continue to do as they are told.

Identification is also common in organizations. The most high profile examples are CEOs or senior management who have gained celebrity status in their companies. Staff will tend to align to individuals who stand out as being successful, are star performers or are on management fast tracks.

An example of internalization is the successful embedding of a company culture. It is most noticeable when you try to make a change. If you implement say a new process for managing and reporting safety standards, then to ensure that the whole organization implements it, right from the CEO to the operations floor, you need to make sure that the belief and new values have been internalized.

Methods of Influence

If someone does not want to do something, then all you can do is influence them into agreeing with you to take a certain course of action or belief. Some will naturally have the ability to influence others, but you can develop your ability through practice. Simple changes can make a difference, for example, dressing smartly for your job and in a way that shows that you are taking your work seriously. You may improve your reputation and credibility through further qualifications and developing your expertise in certain areas. The table below sets out some practical methods of influence.

Table 2.3   A summary of the techniques of influence

Charisma	Influence through personality, success at work, wealth.
Reputation	Influence based on credibility, expertise and built on trust.
Bully pulpit	Influence through fame, celebrity or job status .
Peer pressure	Influence through the use of the desire to fit in with others.
Centre of influence	Influence through the use of influential individuals.

APPLICATION

When faced with a challenging project situation, by a need to rally the troops or to influence decision making, having some structure around methodologies of influence can be useful. Influence involves affecting the actions and thoughts of others. It can be useful in the following situations:

- Acquiring approval for work,

- Engaging teams to deliver tasks,

- During a training session,

- During a sales pitch, and

- Managing people.

You need to find ways that work for you and the audience that you are trying to influence. Your charisma may work with some, and with others you may need to try other techniques such as trading on your reputation, using your status, making use of your authority within the hierarchy, or even through creating an atmosphere of peer pressure. Different methods will work in different environments and you will need to have a feel for what works best with the people you are working with.

Charisma

Charisma can be used to gain power or influence over others. It can take a number of different forms. Attractive people may not always influence based simply on their good looks. Confidence and self esteem can be the by-products of looking (and feeling) good and these can give the charismatic person influence over others. It is not necessarily what you think of yourself but how others perceive you that matters. If you are perceived as having charisma by someone, then they should be open to your influence.

In a project environment, people who are high earners or have a senior role will tend to exert more influence on the basis of this success. Fast tracked employees and star performers can also exert influence in this way.

Reputation

Reputation is one method of influence that you can develop for yourself. This includes using your perceived expertise, credibility and trustworthiness to exert influence. Being reliable, dependable, knowledgeable, helpful and a good listener can all support the development of your ability to influence others. Building up relevant experience is another way of enhancing your reputation.

On a project, you hope to be perceived as someone with the knowledge, experience and confidence to get the job done, an expert resource. You want to be perceived as trustworthy, reliable and able to hit the ground running. This reputation can be built through proactively managing your behaviour at work to support this aim. A damaged reputation, however, will certainly compromise your effectiveness.

Bully pulpit

When you have access to the media or to communication channels through which you can influence people over whom you have no actual power, then this is called using the bully pulpit. Politicians, for example, influence policies over which they may not have an actual say using this technique. Celebrities can use this method to raise awareness for charities they believe in. In this way, they are making use of their influence over their many fans to get their message heard and acted upon.

In a project environment, you can also use this tactic of influence, for example, by bringing in an expert resource or an influential member of the organization that is not directly connected to the project. Sometimes seeing who else is backing and believing in the project can be a useful motivational tool. CEOs, project sponsors, project champions, and external experts can all be considered potential sources of help for utilizing this method of influence.

Peer pressure

This method of influence relies on convincing somebody to do something simply to fit in with a particular group. Peer pressure can make people do things that they may not necessarily believe in or agree with, but they will conform because they feel it is a necessary action to be allowed and accepted into the group.

Peer pressure can be positively applied within a project environment. If, for example, you are rolling part of a project out to various departments, then the fact that you may already have a number of departments on board that are showing positive results can affect attitudes towards the project. These stories can help create enthusiasm and determination to get involved from other parts of the organization. In this way, the remaining teams may feel that they are the only ones not complying with how the rest of the company is moving forward. They would not wish to be left behind.

Centre of influence

We've looked at different ways to influence people and you may think that you are good at some of those methods or have identified people that you know or work with who are good at influencing others. Another tool which is useful is that of the centre of influence. These are people who tend to be the ones that others follow, by watching what they do and how they do it. They seem to lead the way by influencing people either directly or indirectly. It could be by what they buy or even what they believe in and how they live. The key is that it is the perception of others that they are the leaders in the way things are done. Centres of influence are normally willing to try new products, processes and systems, then pass on the information about their successes down into the groups within which they operate.

This model holds true in a business context, where centres of influence can be excellent networkers and have influence over a wider range of people than others and may be good at using indirect control methods. They can be extremely useful when you come up against challenging communication and engagement issues. For example, they may:

- Have a strong network that they can call upon,

- Be good at using the other techniques of influence,

- Resolve issues diplomatically, and

- Connect you with others that can help.

When networking with centres of influence you should use all of the techniques as you would with others, but make sure that you make an extra effort to signal to them that you are aware of their value. This will support the building of a strong relationship with them.

- Give them special treatment,

- Keep them updated,

- Surprise them regularly through genuine contact,

- Help them to expand their network by arranging for them to meet your contacts,

- Try to get together in person on a regular basis, and

- Make sure you recognize their contribution.

In the workplace, it can be critical to identify who are the centres of influence around you. You never know when you will need to call upon their help, guidance or access to contacts. They can be the gatekeepers of information and relationships.

3

Behavioural Models

Gaining an understanding of the behavioural models presented in this chapter can help to make the best use of the resources available by assigning tasks appropriately. They can be used to interpret behaviour and direct ways in which to work more effectively. The Belbin team inventory looks at various preferred ways of working that people adopt in the work place. These are classified as completer finishers, coordinators, implementers, monitor evaluators, plants, resource investigators, shapers, specialists and team workers. This model is not meant to be used to categorize individuals into a role; instead it rates individuals on each of the classes to identify their different strengths. This information can then be used to assign tasks to match these strengths.

When you have teams working together then it is possible to see patterns of behaviour appearing. Sometimes these can have more negative consequences than positive. For example, organizational anti-patterns are patterns of behaviour that groups like project teams can fall into. You may already be familiar with patterns such as analysis paralysis, cash cow, vendor lock-in and design by committee. Recognizing anti-pattern behaviour can aid the evaluation of situations and possibly avert issues as they arise.

Tactics such as career management, business relationship management and short-termism are also discussed as examples of behavioural models that can help in the evaluation of situations. This is particularly useful when a person's behaviour does not match the job that they are supposed to be doing. An example is that once on a project, people can behave in a way to manage their progression and access to promotions and sometimes this can be at odds with their assigned tasks. In fact, it is even possible for people to manage their careers in the opposite way to ensure that they are *not* considered for taking on greater responsibility. Not everyone manages their behaviour so proactively, but some do and it can be helpful to recognize that.

You can also proactively manage and improve your business relationships. As with all other relationships, business relationships can be nurtured and developed to make your working life and delivery of your tasks more enjoyable and rewarding. It is more conducive to work with people that you get on with and trust than to work with people who you find difficult. Being aware of relationship building techniques can help you to strengthen your own working relationships.

Short-termism is a concept taken from politics and it can be usefully applied to project situations. It is a particular risk when people are involved in a project for a finite time and wish to leave unpleasant activities for others to deal with.

Belbin Team Inventory

The Belbin team inventory is a behavioural tool that can be used to understand how individuals behave in a team environment (Belbin, 1993). This is achieved through a combination of self evaluation and how your team views you. Myers-Briggs focused on placing individuals into one of 16 categories or types, whereas the Belbin model looks at rating each individual on their behaviour against each of the nine roles within the model. Each individual can have a strong preference even in multiple roles. No one role is exclusive to another. Indeed, a person can try to influence their role through conscious effort, training and development. These nine roles are described in the table below. Further information can be found in Belbin Associates (2009) and Belbin (2003).

Table 3.1   A summary of the nine Belbin team roles

Coordinator	Completer Finisher	Implementer
Likes to take charge and be responsible for delegating tasks. Good at identifying who will be good for taking on which task. Natural leader and behaves in a confident manner. Ensures that everyone understands what they have to do. Able to delegate effectively. Can be perceived as off-loading their work.	Thoroughly completes work, checking and double checking. Produces high quality output. Can get frustrated at others' lack of perfectionism. Uncomfortable with trusting others to do as good a job as them. Finds delegation difficult.	Takes direction well. Turns ideas into plans of action and focuses on delivery. Takes on tasks that others avoid. Can be frustrating to work with as they use their own preferred methods .

Monitor Evaluator	Plants	Resource Investigator
Evaluates situations logically and objectively. Puts forward their independent ideas . Considers all relevant information and takes time over decision making. Often uses an analytical approach. Can be perceived as dispassionate about their work and hence demotivates others.	Generates ideas and innovative solutions to problems. Prefers to look at the big picture rather than get involved in the details. Can be enthusiastic about their proposals. Can find it difficult to communicate their ideas to others.	Full of enthusiasm and motivation at the beginning of a project. Keen to find and pursue opportunities. Make good sales people. Not good at generating their own ideas. Happy to find and use ideas and methodologies of others. Can be excellent networkers as is needed for gathering the ideas of others. Can lose momentum and enthusiasm closer to the end of the project. Not focused on details.
Shaper	**Specialist**	**Team worker**
Focuses on delivering the desired outcome. Full of energy and enthusiasm. Can get frustrated with others not as enthusiastic as themselves. Influences and shapes others into achieving the team goal. Can come across as challenging and argumentative. Multiple shapers in a team can lead to conflict.	Experts in their specific fields. Enjoys working with others when they are in their comfort zone. Happy to educate and train people by sharing their wisdom. Happy to learn something new as long as it is within their subject area. Can bring a high level of skill to a team. Uncomfortable outside their area of expertise.	Works effectively with other people through the use of their diplomatic skills. Good at smoothing over conflict. Can act as a go between for those that don't get on together. Finds it difficult to make decisions and to take sides.

APPLICATION

In the workplace, it is rare for such roles and characteristics of individuals to be taken into account during staffing. However, as you can see from the descriptions in the table, you may recognize traits of your team members in the role definitions. Again, when there is conflict on a project or you are finding it difficult to get something communicated or a task delivered, then it can be worthwhile reviewing the table of roles and seeing whether you are behaving in a way that is most likely to ensure your requests are received in the most constructive way for the individuals involved. A lot of the success on projects relies on people working together, and most teams by their very nature tend to be thrown together with resources that were available. The dream team that would be ideal for delivering the project is rarely one that can be practically drawn together.

Even though people may not fit into these roles exactly, and indeed this model is supposed to rate people on their tendency towards each role rather than actually categorizing them, it is useful to be aware that people work in different ways. All individuals on a project bring something unique to the team. They will each have their preferred way of working and their strengths that they can contribute to the team. If you are the project manager, then you should give people appropriate tasks and roles that draw upon their strengths and fit in with yours.

Organizational Anti-Patterns

The concept of anti-patterns was originally developed in software engineering, but it has been usefully applied to behaviours in organizations. Anti-patterns, also known as pitfalls or dark patterns, are repeated patterns of action that, although appearing to be beneficial, have more negative than positive consequences. You may have come across many of these behavioural patterns at work and some common anti-patterns are described in Table 3.2 below. Further information can be found in Brown et al. (1998 and 2000).

Table 3.2   Examples of behavioural anti-patterns observed in organizations

Analysis paralysis	More time is spent on the analysis phase of a project, rather than getting on with delivery.
Authoritarian management	Management with intolerance for others' opinions.
Bystander apathy	A wrong decision is made and yet those who notice it do nothing about it.
Cash cow	A profitable revenue stream that can lead to complacency about developing new products and services.
Death march	Everybody except the project sponsor knowing that the project is going to be a failure.
Design by committee	Too many people involved in the decision making process resulting in a poor but consensual outcome.
Escalation of commitment	Work packages continuing that are no longer required.
Group think (Peer pressure)	Members of a team avoid raising queries that run counter to the prevailing mood of the group.
Mushroom management	Keeping people in the dark by restricting the flow of information.
No moral hazard	The decision maker being isolated from the consequences of their decisions.
Vendor lock-in	Increasing dependency on a vendor due to financial, practical or even knowledge based reasons.

APPLICATION

Being aware of behavioural anti-patterns can enable recognition of potential problems before they arise. Project teams can be particularly susceptible to anti-pattern behaviour and so acknowledgement of the situation can make it easier to combat any negative consequences.

Tactics

CAREER MANAGEMENT

Some people will be happy with where they are in their careers, whilst others will be carefully and proactively managing their career to position themselves for advancement. It can be important to be aware of career management tactics in play, as this can affect behaviour in an otherwise unexpected way. For some, once they have a job, they no longer actively pursue promotion or more responsibility. If it comes along then great and even if it doesn't, then maybe they weren't quite good enough in their own mind. Others may continuously and actively manage their careers even after they have got the job, by continuing to search for opportunities inside the organization. The table below describes a number of common career management tactics. Further information can be found in Yarnell (2007) and Cross and Hailstone (2007).

Table 3.3   Examples of career management tactics

1. Continually searching for opportunities to develop.	This may be exhibited by seeking chances to take on more responsibility, training and qualifications, and this individual will continue to strengthen their resume.
2. Networking and building relationships both internally and externally.	A networker stays in touch with former colleagues when either the networker or their contact leaves the company. The networker tries to stay in touch regularly by sharing news, insights and information. They let others know about their expanding experience and network.
3. Keeping up to date with the latest news in the industry.	This will help them to put project objectives into a larger context and also to draw upon this breadth of relevant knowledge as appropriate. This can help them to innovate and bring something extra to the table at work.
4. Developing their area of skills and expertise to remain as marketable as possible.	Many take evening or weekend courses or self-learn new skills.
5. Joining professional associations and reading trade journals.	They may even try to get more involved with those organizations through writing articles, giving presentations or standing for committee positions. By doing this, they enhance their own reputation and often also that of your firm.

Application

Sometimes project requirements may be directly in conflict with the personal objectives of an individual. The tactics listed above represent examples where people are looking to advance their careers. Equally, you may be affected by some tactics with different objectives such as not wanting any kind of career progression and actively avoiding it. In this case, traits that you may see include:

- Avoiding greater responsibility,

- Satisfaction in their current role,

- Preferring to increase depth of knowledge rather than breadth, and

- Dislike of drawing attention.

You need to be alert to these behaviours, whether positive or negative. For example, your project may appeal to a career manager and so you may be able to use their ambition and enthusiasm to win support for your plans.

BUSINESS RELATIONSHIP MANAGEMENT

Delivering projects is easier if you are good at building relationships. Some people are natural relationship builders, others are unconscious relationship destroyers. You need to work with other people, and if you get on, then getting tasks completed will be easier and more enjoyable. You also need to trust other people with whom you are working. Creating an open and trusting environment will enable your team to work together more effectively. Managing your business relationships is an essential skill. The better you are at this, the easier it will be for you to work with others and to deliver on projects. Further information can be found in Ford et al. (2003).

You can develop your relationship building and networking skills through techniques such as:

- Keeping in touch with colleagues,

- Connecting people even when there is no personal benefit to be gained,

- Following up quickly and reliably,

- Being genuine in your communications and developing friendships,

- Making others feel comfortable, and

- Regularly making useful contact.

Application

Excellent networking and relationship building skills are an essential part of a project manager's toolkit. This can make all of the tasks far more pleasant and easier to achieve if your relationship management skills are good. These skills can also be useful for:

- Negotiating deals,

- Mediating issues within the team,

- Developing the ability to work with all kinds of individuals,

- Meeting new people and working effectively with them right from the start, and

- Developing trust.

There are a number of ways that can make your relationships stronger, for example, when you are delegating tasks, or leading people they have to buy into you and not just your instructions. The more easily they can buy into you, the easier it will be for them to buy into your ideas, concepts, products and services. So there is no point in necessarily drowning them in information and detail that can be done outside of a meeting. Also being able to gain the trust of other people will enable them to count on you.

SHORT-TERMISM

Short-termism is an effect that can often be seen in political situations. Governing parties tend to have a defined and finite term of office and this can affect their decision making. It can lead to making changes that have short term benefits that will take effect during their term so that they can reap the rewards. This can be at the cost of not making decisions based on the longer term benefits, especially if those benefits or returns will not show for many years after their term has come to an end. In fact, in the short term these decisions based on long term benefits may have negative consequences, for example, upfront costs and investments or a short term rise in unemployment. Further information can be found in Peppers et al. (2008).

Application

This same effect is seen in organizations. When individuals know that they are about to move on to something else at some definite time in the future, then they may run projects in a way that reflects this. For example, a project manager may delay difficult decisions and conversations for the new incoming project manager, particularly, in the case where there may be short term unpleasantness that could be passed onto somebody else. Managing employee discipline and grievances often falls into this category. Delaying problems to pass them onto somebody else is common practice, particularly in project environments where the composition of the project team can be fluid and likely to change, or as you go from one project phase to the next.

4

Communication Models

There are people who are strong communicators and you may wonder what it is about the way that they communicate that makes them so successful. Studies have been performed on types of communication transactions. These can help you identify how people are communicating and how best they might be engaged with. The background behind two communication models is described, namely, neuro-linguistic programming (NLP) and transactional analysis (TA). The first studied successful patterns of communication. The latter considered conversational transactions and how they can have different meanings depending on the classification of the transactional type.

Neuro-Linguistic Programming (NLP)

Neuro-linguistic programming is a model of communication based on observing successful patterns of communication between people (Bandler and Grinder, 1989). Based on these observations, NLP explores ways of increasing people's awareness of the quality of their communication and improving their communication techniques. It is often viewed as a self help methodology. The title, NLP, was created to give the sense of a theoretical connection between neurological processes, language and behavioural patterns that have been learned through experience, hence the programming in the name. The basis of their theory was observations of what made successful communicators.

NLP was originally promoted by its founders, Bandler and Grinder, in the 1970s as an effective form of psychological therapy, capable of addressing the full range of problems which psychologists are likely to encounter, such as phobias, depression, habit disorder, psychosomatic illnesses and learning disorders. Later, it was promoted as scientific modelling of how successful or outstanding people in different fields obtain their results. NLP could be learned by anyone to improve their effectiveness both personally and professionally. Where NLP has been successful is in the self help market and life coaching arenas. The model was based on the observations described below. Further information can be found in Molden (2007), Knight (2002), Basu (2009) and O'Connor and Seymour (2003).

THE BASIS OF NEURO-LINGUISTIC MODELLING: CONCLUSIONS FROM THE OBSERVATIONS OF SUCCESSFUL PEOPLE

1. Focus on their objective, ensuring that their activities directly contribute to their goal. They do not get easily side-tracked.
2. Open to trying new approaches. The goal mattered rather than the route taken to achieve it.
3. Good at recognizing and responding to both verbal and non-verbal communication.
4. Saw challenges on the route to their goal as opportunities to develop their skills.
5. Considered others as working in the best way that they knew rather than judging them as being wrong in some way.
6. Noticed certain situations effortlessly.
7. Worked persistently and paid attention to detail.
8. Approached new challenges by gathering information until they felt knowledgeable enough to start making changes of their own.

These observations were used by Bandler and Grinder to draw some basic conclusions about successful behaviour patterns. They came up with three rules that would lead to successful communication in business and sales environments. First, that you should know what outcome you want and be flexible in your approach to achieving it. Second, that you should test what kind of response you get when using different kinds of behaviour. And finally, that you need to be able to recognise when you eventually get the response that met your objective.

THE THREE BEHAVIOUR PATTERNS FROM NLP THAT UNDERPIN SUCCESSFUL COMMUNICATION

1. To know what outcome you want and to be flexible in your behaviour and ways to achieve it.
2. To test the water with different kinds of behaviour in order to find out what response you get with each approach.
3. To have enough experience to notice when you get the response that you were after.

APPLICATION

In contrast to mainstream psychotherapy, NLP does not concentrate on the diagnosis, treatment and assessment of mental and behavioural disorders. Instead, it focuses on helping clients to overcome their own self-perceived problems. NLP tries to do this in the context of being aware of your own capabilities. Some people find that NLP has benefits in the workplace as it can help them to prepare and deliver higher impact communications. The key to NLP techniques is to take in both verbal and non-verbal communication effectively and respond to it in kind. The benefits of using NLP in a project context include:

- Focusing on the project vision and not getting side tracked,

- Creating a rapport with both individuals and groups,

- Improving the ability to manage conflict and disagreements, and

- Effectively monitoring relationships with other people.

Sometimes issues on a project arise simply due to miscommunication and misunderstandings. You may find that communication models, such as NLP, may help you improve your communication techniques.

Transactional Analysis (TA)

Transactional analysis is an integrative approach to the theory of psychology and psychotherapy developed by Eric Berne in the 1950s. Transactional analysis is a theory of personality and systematic psychotherapy for personal growth and personal change. It has been used in a number of different ways and some of these are described below.

1.   As a theory of personality, it categorizes and models people in order to understand how they function and express themselves. The ego state model described later is an example of this.

2.   As a theory of communication and used in the context of analysing and managing systems and also organizations.

3.   As a theory of child development.

4.   Transactional analysis introduced the concept of a life story, also called a life script. A life script describes how each person perceives their own life and how they understand what matters to them and what type of person they are.

5.   TA can be used in the diagnosis and treatment of psychological disorders and also in the counselling of both individuals and groups.

6.   In business and in education, TA has been used as a method of keeping communication clear and appropriate to the level and context in which it is being used.

Transactional analysis emphasizes a pragmatic approach based on what works and as such it is continually evolving. However, some of the main concepts are described below.

THE EGO-STATE (OR PARENT-ADULT-CHILD) MODEL

At any given time, a person experiences and manifests their personality through a mix of behaviours, thoughts and feelings. Typically, according to transactional analysis, there are three ego states that people consistently use and these are shown in the table below.

Table 4.1   The three ego states according to Transactional Analysis

Parent	A state in which people behave, feel, and think in response to an unconscious mimicking of how their parents (or other parental figures) acted, or how they interpreted their parent's actions. Typically, parental ego states are evidenced by behaviours that are judgemental; finger wagging or critical generalizations of a group or an individual show someone who is communicating in the parent state.

Adult	A state of the ego which is most rational, processing information and making predictions that while not absent of major emotions, shows awareness of emotion and of its impact. Communicating in this ego state, and encouraging others to respond in a similar way, is one of the aims of a good communicator.
Child	A state in which people behave, feel and think as they did in childhood. For example, a person who receives a poor evaluation at work may respond by looking at the floor, and crying or pouting, as they used to when scolded as a child. Conversely, a person who receives a good evaluation may respond with a broad smile and a joyful gesture of thanks. The positive elements of the child ego state are associated with emotions, creation, recreation, spontaneity and intimacy.

These ego states can represent the actual relationships that are under consideration. Transactional analysis is applied to the business environment by considering how and when people take on the three roles of parent, adult or child, as described above. For example, a project manager may take on the role of a parent by moaning at a member of the team and the team member may respond by apologizing profusely as if they were in a childlike state. Further information on transactional analysis can be found in Stewart and Joines (1987), Steiner (1990), Berne (2001) and Stewart (2007).

You can identify the ego state that a person is communicating from by observing them and by building up your experience of them. Each ego state is considered to manifest itself uniquely in each individual. This is because everybody has a different experience of childhood, their relationship with their parents and their ideas of how an adult should behave.

TRANSACTIONS AND STROKES

A transaction refers to the dialogue, both spoken and unspoken, that takes place between people. Often unspoken psychological communication may run parallel to verbal communication. Transactional analysis considers the ego states that people are in when they are communicating. Sometimes one person's ego state matches that of the other person and sometimes it does not. When the ego states are not complementary, then they may give rise to misunderstandings or misinterpretations of intentions.

The term strokes refers to the response or recognition that one person gives another. People tend to look for positive strokes or responses to their communication, and when they fail to receive a positive stroke they may even settle for a negative stroke. The idea is that people desire recognition and if they cannot get positive recognition then even negative recognition will suffice.

People tend to solicit responses on the basis of their ego state. A child may solicit a parental response and vice versa. Take for example a project manager with an authoritarian style. They may expect people to respond submissively, as a child would, and they may seek to punish those who do not conform to this behaviour.

The important thing to remember is that people prefer to have transactions with other people. This is considered fundamental to human nature. This is the reason why they may be happy to settle for negative transactions rather than no transaction at all. A transaction is termed positive or negative based on the nature of the strokes that take place within the transaction. Thus, for some project team members, getting shouted at by the project manager may be preferred to simply being ignored by them.

APPLICATION

Complementary transactions involve both parties responding by correctly identifying and addressing the ego state that the other is in. Some examples are given using the familiar project management environment.

COMPLEMENTARY TRANSACTIONS

Example 1: Adult to Adult

Project manager:	'How long do you think this task should take?'
Task owner:	'Based on past experience, I believe it should take about five days to deliver.'
Project manager:	'Okay. Thanks for the information. I'll get that into the overall plan.'

Example 2: Child to Child

Project manager:	'Do you think anyone will notice if we don't attend this meeting? Shall we go and play golf instead this afternoon?'
Project team member:	'That sounds really good. The weather is really great. Do you know where we can go?'

Example 3: Parent to Child and Child to Parent

Project manager: 'You should have finished that report by now.' (Parent to Child)

Project team member: 'Could you stop moaning at me? I'll get it done in time for the deadline, don't worry.' (Child to Parent)

Crossed transactions can result in a failure to communicate effectively because each person is communicating from an ego state that is not compatible. For this reason, the message can be misinterpreted and cause unnecessary frustration. An example of this is given below, where a project manager is following up on how a task is progressing using an adult to adult method, however the response comes back in a child to parent form.

CROSSED TRANSACTIONS

Example 1: Adult to Adult and Child to Parent

Project manager: 'How is that task coming along?' (Adult to Adult)

Task owner: 'I told you that I would take care of it. There is no need to keep chasing me.' (Child to Parent)

Example 2: Parent to Child and Adult to Adult

Project manager: 'How long do you really think this task should take?' (Parent to Child)

Task owner: 'Based on past experience, I believe it should take about five days to deliver.' (Adult to Adult)

Project manager: 'I'll put it down as two days, because that's what we need it to be.' (Parent to Child)

Since the objective is to encourage adult to adult transactions, when you are faced with someone communicating from a Parent to Child ego state, you will need to respond as an adult. This would mean that you would deliberately cross transact. You may need to repeat your adult response several times during the exchange before they change ego state. You should also recognize that the nature of human beings means that you may not always successfully engage their adult ego state. Whatever happens, you need to avoid dropping the level of your ego state to match theirs.

Transactional analysis can be a useful way of thinking about how conversations are sometimes misunderstood or misinterpreted. It can help you to understand why perhaps somebody responded in a way that you were not expecting. Project management inevitably requires you to interact with a whole range of individuals, and being aware of the different ways in which people communicate or the different ways in which people perceive your communication may help you resolve conflicts and manage disagreements.

PART II

Case Studies by Project Lifecycle Stage

Quick Reference Guide to the Models of Human Behaviour

Part I focused on introducing a variety of reasonably well known models that you may already be familiar with and that can be used to support in the problem solving of political situations. As a quick reference guide, these concepts are summarized below.

PSYCHOLOGICAL PROFILING

Maslow's theory of human motivation

This is a five-layer model of needs or motivations. As soon as some of these needs are met, then the desire to fulfil new needs arise, leading to a constant feeling of dissatisfaction.

- Level 1: Physiological,

- Level 2: Safety,

- Level 3: Love and belonging,

- Level 4: Self esteem, and

- Level 5: Self actualization.

Myers-Briggs type indicator (MBTI)

This model considers individuals as being either born with or developing certain preferred ways of thinking and acting. It uses a classification system based on eight classes, paired into four opposing pairs. Simply applying the definition of these classes can be useful in highlighting preferred ways of working for different people.

- Attitude preference: Extroversion (act then reflect) or Introversion (reflect then act),

- Information gathering preference: Sensing (data and facts) or Intuition (insight and theories),

- Decision making preference: Thinking (logical) or Feeling (empathy and diplomacy), and

- Lifestyle preference: Judging (prefer decision making to information gathering) or Perceiving (prefer information gathering to decision making).

INFLUENCE

Types of influence

- Soft influence: use of communication and engagement, and

- Hard influence: creation of rules.

Degrees of influence

- Compliance: accepts beliefs only in public,

- Identification: accepts beliefs only under the influence of a leader, and

- Internalization: accepts beliefs both in public and in private.

Methods of influence

- Charisma: Influence through personality, success at work, wealth,

- Reputation: Influence based on credibility, expertise and built on trust,

- Bully pulpit: Influence through fame, celebrity or job status,

- Peer pressure: Influence through the use of the desire to fit in with others, and

- Centre of influence: Influence through the use of influential individuals.

BEHAVIOURAL

Belbin team inventory

This model can be used to identify the strengths and weakness of individuals in different role types.

Coordinator:

- Likes to take charge and be responsible for delegating tasks,

- Good at identifying who will be suitable for each task,

- Natural leader and behaves in a confident manner,

- Ensures that everyone understands what they have to do,

- Able to delegate effectively, and

- Can be perceived as off-loading their work.

Completer finisher:

- Thoroughly completes work, checking and double checking,

- Produces high quality output,

- Can get frustrated at others' lack of perfectionism,

- Uncomfortable with trusting others to do as good a job as them, and

- Finds delegation difficult.

Implementer:

- Takes direction well,

- Turns ideas into plans of action and focuses on delivery,

- Takes on tasks that others avoid, and

- Can be frustrating to work with as they use their own preferred methods.

Monitor evaluator:

- Evaluates situations logically and objectively,

- Puts forward their independent ideas,

- Considers all relevant information and takes time over decision making,

- Often uses an analytical approach, and

- Can be perceived as dispassionate about their work and hence can demotivate others.

Plants:

- Generates ideas and innovative solutions to problems,

- Prefers to look at the big picture rather than get involved in the details,

- Can be enthusiastic about their proposals, and

- Can find it difficult to communicate their ideas to others.

Resource investigator:

- Full of enthusiasm and motivation at the beginning of a project,

- Keen to find and pursue opportunities,

- Make good sales people,

- Not good at generating their own ideas,

- Happy to find and use ideas and methodologies of others,

- Can be excellent networkers as is needed for gathering the ideas of others,

- Can lose momentum and enthusiasm closer to the end of the project, and

- Not focused on details.

Shaper:

- Focuses on delivering the desired outcome,

- Full of energy and enthusiasm,

- Can get frustrated with others not as enthusiastic as themselves,

- Influences and shapes others into achieving the team goal,

- Can come across as challenging and argumentative, and

- Multiple shapers in a team can lead to conflict.

Specialist:

- Experts in their specific fields,

- Enjoys working with others when they are in their comfort zone,

- Happy to educate and train people by sharing their wisdom,

- Happy to learn something new as long as it is within their subject area,

- Can bring a high level of skill to a team, and

- Uncomfortable outside their area of expertise.

Team worker:

- Works effectively with other people through the use of their diplomatic skills,

- Good at smoothing over conflict,

- Can act as a go between for those that don't get on together, and

- Finds it difficult to make decisions and to take sides.

Organizational anti-patterns examples

- Analysis paralysis: More time is spent on the analysis phase of a project, rather than getting on with delivery.

- Authoritarian management: Management with intolerance for others' opinions.

- Bystander apathy: A wrong decision is made and yet those who notice it do nothing about it.

- Cash cow: A profitable revenue stream that can lead to complacency about developing new products and services.

- Death march: Everybody except the project sponsor knowing that the project is going to be a failure.

- Design by committee: Too many people involved in the decision making process resulting in a poor but consensual outcome.

- Escalation of commitment: Work packages continuing that are no longer required.

- Group think (peer pressure): Members of a team avoid raising queries that run counter to the prevailing mood of the group.

- Mushroom management: Keeping people in the dark by restricting the flow of information.

- No moral hazard: The decision maker being isolated from the consequences of their decisions.

- Vendor lock-in: Increasing dependency on a vendor due to financial, practical or even knowledge based reasons.

Examples of tactics

- Career management: behaving in a way to progress ones career rather than focusing on the delivery of the given job.

- Business relationship management (networking): actively nurturing relationships that could be of mutual benefit.

- Short-termism: Focusing on short term effects only rather than overall objectives.

COMMUNICATION

Neuro-linguistic programming (NLP)

Using the patterns of communication identified in successful communicators.

- Know what outcome you want and be flexible in the method of its achievement,

- Test the water with different kinds of behaviour to establish the response you get with each approach, and

- Develop enough experience to notice when you get the desired response.

Transactional analysis (TA)

A transaction refers to the dialogue, both spoken and unspoken, that takes place between people. Often unspoken psychological communication may run parallel to verbal communication. Transactional analysis considers the ego state that people are in when they are communicating. Sometimes one person's ego state matches that of the other person and sometimes it does not. When the ego states are not complementary, then they may give rise to misunderstandings or misinterpretations of intentions.

Template for Assessing Political Situations

The fundamentals of each of these concepts were described in Part I. They can be used to structure your analysis of political situations and to generate options for resolution. When considering a particular political situation, you can use the quick reference guide to identify which of the concepts may be applicable. The template opposite can then be used for jotting down your notes.

Appropriate Models	Notes
Psychological profiling	
Influence	
Behaviour	
Communication	

The chapters in Part II focus on each stage of the project lifecycle. These are: Chapter 5 'Project Definition', Chapter 6 'Planning and Risk Management', Chapter 7 'Implementation', Chapter 8 'Project Evaluation and Closure'.

It is assumed that the reader is mostly conversant with project management methodologies and so these are only briefly described. Case studies considering typical political situations are discussed. The template is then used as a starting point for assessing these cases. Potential options for identifying solutions are noted in the template. One or more of these options is then explored in greater detail for each case. Thus the case studies are used to demonstrate how a light touch approach of the theoretical concepts can provide greater insight and present ways to move forward.

5

Project Definition

Introduction

PROJECT CONCEPTION

A project is normally first conceived on the basis of some business need having emerged. There may have been a clearly defined option evaluation and selection phase prior to project conception, during which various options were assessed and a business case produced. Sometimes that phase can be brief and at other times it may take months or years to complete. The resulting project business case should contain an overview of the project requirements. Once the business case has been approved, the project can then be detailed further, thus entering the project definition phase. This phase involves preparing sufficient information to get the project started.

The individuals involved in the evaluation of potential project options are often not the same individuals involved in owning and implementing the project further down the line. The project team should understand the intent under which a particular project direction was selected and the criteria that were applied. If the project team is lucky enough to have been involved in the early stages of project development, then they will need to be aware of any change in requirements as the project progresses into implementation. Further information about this stage of the project can be found in Nokes and Kelly (2007), Posner and Applegarth (2008), Lock (2007) and Reiss (2007).

PROJECT DEFINITION DOCUMENT

Creating some form of a project definition document is a standard methodology for starting a project. This document is also often called the project charter or a terms of reference document. It does not need to be a lengthy report, but it should be sufficiently detailed to provide a framework for the implementation of the project. It is good practice to have in mind what kind of document or report you want to emerge from this exercise. In the briefest form, the project definition document should contain a little bit about the background of the project and why it has come about and a definition of what the problem is that the project is trying to resolve or the product, system, process or service that is intended to be the output. It should lay out the project scope and the main objectives.

By this stage, there should also be a clear understanding of who the key stakeholders are and how they are linked and contributing to the project. Additionally, it makes sense to have something written down about the various roles and responsibilities to avoid any confusion. An organization chart can be useful here, focusing on those involved in the project and how they inter-relate from the project perspective. The chart does not necessarily need to take into account operational roles or the relative grades outside of the project environment.

To summarize, the key components of a project definition document are:

- Background to the project and/or its business case,

- Project objectives,

- Project organization chart,

- Outline of roles and responsibilities,

- Budget and resources allocation, and

- Plan.

This definition document often goes on to form a key reference point for the project. If your project has started off without a charter or project definition document, it can still be useful to compile one since it has many uses going forward including reporting. It can also form a simple induction for new team members, giving them all the relevant information.

PROJECT STAKEHOLDERS

During this project stage, the team is probably still being compiled and it represents an opportunity to understand the rationale of the individuals who are brought on board. It is at this stage of defining the project and the project team that you can begin to realize that there is both an official project team made up of those responsible for the delivery and an unofficial project team of decision makers who may not appear on the project organization chart. It is important to understand that the official and unofficial project teams are not identical and may involve little overlap. Understanding the motivations of both sets of stakeholders at this stage is critical to ensuring their buy-in. This definition stage typically involves senior managers who are unlikely to be part of the actual implementation. However, without the strong engagement of these individuals it can be difficult to deliver a project successfully. The greater the number of stakeholders and the larger the size of the official and unofficial project teams, the greater the risk that personal or organizational politics will undermine the objectives and implementation of the project.

STAFFING ISSUES

Pulling together the team to get the project going often begins around the time that the project definition document is being put in place or shortly after. The project may consist of a number of different phases with different staffing requirements or it may be that as the project progresses different groups of people and stakeholders naturally become involved. Political situations around project staffing and issues between various stakeholder groups can arise at any time in the project; from initiation to the point of project completion. This chapter looks at some of the political situations that can arise based specifically around the staffing and interaction of the project team. Further information about staffing can be found in Bechet (2008), Stanford (2007) and Emmerichs (2003).

COMMUNICATION AND THE PROJECT TEAM

The project team comprises the project manager and those that report directly to them. The responsibilities of the project team include project planning and scheduling; communication; monitoring and control; budgeting; problem and conflict identification and resolution and quality control. The project manager needs to ensure that they use resources efficiently, keep management informed and adhere to agreed policies and procedures. In addition, the project manager has responsibilities to the project team, including: keeping the project on target, providing appropriate resources, coordinating the team and providing support. Many projects will also involve a number of stakeholders outside the project team itself. The project manager may need to report in to a project board or project steering committee. There may also be a separate project sponsor and project owner involved. The project team will need to collaborate with any teams that support the project; suppliers of products and services to the project and potentially even the users and customers of the project's end results. Not all projects will have all of the positions and often the same individuals may take on several responsibilities.

Project politics are not only the concern of the project manager. They can affect all members of the project team and all members need to be able to recognize and deal with them. Having an appreciation for the politics involved on a project enables effective working. In the simplest of examples, it will help to:

- Manage expectations,

- Control the flow of information,

- Recognize how to best deal with others, and

- Understand behaviours.

INTERACTIONS

As a project team member, you will need to interact with most, if not all, of the stakeholders, either directly or indirectly. You may be purchasing products or services for the project, or you may be responsible for defining the requirements and finding suppliers. How important the interaction is with each stakeholder group on your project will depend on the nature of your project and also the accessibility of the individual groups. It may be beneficial to communicate in depth with the users, for example, however this may not be possible or even preferable in reality.

As a project team member, you will always need to make a judgement as to who the important stakeholders are, which of them you can influence and how they can make a difference. You may find that you do this intuitively or you may need to reflect and plan how to move forward. The important groups may change as the project progresses or as the situation changes. One of the most important aspects in terms of completing a project successfully will rely on your ability to engage the right people at the right time. You may not always get it right the first time and it is likely to prove to be a continuing process, however, this engagement will make the running of the project far smoother.

There are many reasons why you may not necessarily be able to involve the best people in the project, for example, they may:

- Have left the firm,

- Be in demand on another project,

- Be geographically inaccessible,

- Be on leave, and

- Have confidentiality constraints.

You will need to be aware of how stakeholders are engaged with your project both on paper and in reality. If they are very busy, then it may be possible to tag a delegated individual who can substitute for them for the purpose of day-to-day contact, leaving the actual stakeholder to be contacted only for more critical matters. Tactics for managing this situation include:

- Identifying an appropriate contact point,

- Raising the profile of your project on their radar, and

- Being persistent.

Sometimes an apparent cold shoulder (or indeed a failure to respond at all) may simply be evidence of their overwhelming workload rather than a lack of enthusiasm for your project. Avoid making assumptions about their attitude towards your project.

SUMMARY OF TOPICS

Various situations can arise at this early stage of project definition and the models presented in Part I can be used to analyse them and to generate options for resolution. The course of action then chosen will depend to a large extent on the particulars of the situation and individuals involved. Take for example, Myers-Briggs type indicator that can be used to give a sense of the personalities involved on the project and it may help you to anticipate how they might react under various conditions. The Belbin team inventory can give you an idea of the types of personalities involved and to identify the strengths and weaknesses in your team. Identifying centres of influence will help you to get tasks delivered. Being aware of the career management tactics being used will help explain why certain people behave in a particular way. The topics considered in this chapter are outlined below.

Establishing the project background:

- Using the story for motivation, and

- Controlling the project design.

Redirecting the project:

- Evaluating options, and

- Risking a new supplier.

Working with key stakeholders:

- Stakeholders aspirations,

- Influencing stakeholders, and

- The organization chart.

Establishing the Project Background

USING THE STORY FOR MOTIVATION

It can be useful to find out what the original and *real* underlying reason was behind a project. If you start looking into the background of a project, you may find that there was a serious issue, either within the company or something that happened in another company that set your project in motion. Such a story can be a useful method of motivating people on your project through the demonstration of the value of their work. This is particularly the case if your team view your project as being a tick in the box kind of exercise.

This knowledge can help you direct the project or at the very least give you a better context. The *real* reasons for the project may not be transparent, perhaps, because the originators have moved on to new roles. There may, for example, have been a newsworthy event that spurred the organization into action. High profile stories of business risks tend to have an energizing effect causing organizations to reflect inwards.

CASE STUDY: DATA LOSS LEADING TO A PROJECT

Take the example of the accidental loss of confidential information (such as personal, medical, or even bank account details), which leads to a project. Such information, concerning sometimes numerous individuals, may be lost in transit, stolen on a laptop or inadvertently transmitted to an inappropriate party. Not only would the organization that lost the data wish to make changes to ensure that such an event is not repeated, it could also encourage other companies to learn from these mistakes and proactively evaluate their procedures and systems to ensure that they don't make the same error.

Due to the embarrassing nature of the situation, management may not wish to inform staff about the reasons for the project. However, the story could be used to motivate the delivery team and improve adoption of new data protection processes by the organization.

Table 5.1 Case study analysis: Data loss leading to a project

Appropriate models	Notes
Psychological profiling	People like to feel that they are valued and trusted. This improves their self esteem and directly addresses the self esteem level as described by Maslow. The background story of the project could be used as a key motivational tool.
Influence	If the project team needs to roll out new processes in order to combat future leaks of information, then a positive implementation of peer pressure could be applied in order to seek faster adoption. This could be achieved by setting positive examples to follow.
Behaviour	This is a situation where mushroom management (anti-patterns) is in play, where only the senior people have key information. Unless confidentiality is a problem, it could be beneficial to share the background, since most people like to understand why they are being asked to perform certain tasks.
Communication	Using transactional analysis, communicating the issues in an adult way should show people that you trust and respect them. This should make them feel valued and therefore more satisfied in their efforts on the project as well as having an improved appreciation of the risks to data security. It should also encourage an adult response to the uptake of new processes.

Issues such as loss of data can occur at any time and so you need to be prepared to deal with them, whilst minimizing any negative impact. It is best to proactively manage the disclosure and reassure people that such a problem will not arise again. Probing into the source of the project's inception can provide unique insight. At the very least, the background can form a story used to motivate and inspire. Inevitably, team members will want to know the justification for the project and understand how their contribution adds value. This is linked into the basic needs as described in Maslow's theory of motivation. If the project happens to be highly confidential then this can act to make the team feel even more important and in effect motivate them further.

Establishing the project need can be achieved through, for example:

- Interviewing key stakeholders,

- Delving into the project paperwork and communications, and

- Researching similar cases and their solutions externally.

Once the information has been collected on the reason that the project was initiated, you will need to decide how best to compile that information into a form that can be used for engagement. This does not have to be a lengthy document. A one-page briefing format or a couple of slides could be sufficient to describe the chronological steps that occurred leading to the project. This summary should answer all the key questions and provide the right level of supporting data to be able to stand alone and be used easily for distribution or for communication when required. It should make sense to somebody outside of the project and so you should try not to use too much internal jargon.

CONTROLLING THE PROJECT DESIGN

At the start of the project there may be many senior individuals within the organization involved. They will all have their own angle on what the project should deliver and how, as they will all want to ensure that their team, department or organization realizes as many benefits as possible from the project. You may need to have many people involved simply because without them it will not be possible to implement the project successfully. If the group of stakeholders becomes large then there is a risk of design by committee. Unless there is clarity around roles and responsibilities amongst stakeholders and the project team, there is a risk that too many people will be involved directly in the decision making. This can lead to frustration with unclear project objectives and far from optimal outcomes that are reached by consensus.

CASE STUDY: WIDENING PROJECT SCOPE

In this example, senior management were having trouble keeping on top of the activity in the company. They were ultimately responsible for a large number of projects, of differing types and budgets. Most projects required collaboration between different parts of the business and establishing coordination to minimize any duplication of effort was key. A system to oversee all the activity was needed so that they could make more meaningful contributions and interventions. It was agreed that a web based project reporting system would be able to resolve the issues, by enabling the coordination of the portfolio. The system was to be populated by the project teams and senior management would be able to create reports from the system.

The problem with such a solution was that without a clear specification it would be difficult to deliver. In this case study, many stakeholders had an interest in the system and wished to have input on the design. If each stakeholder did not have their requests implemented then the uptake of the new system into their teams would be impossible. As a result the web based solution was designed by a large committee. Software feature requests and demands were made by each stakeholder. Feature requests continued to be made during implementation that could not be denied as they were deal breakers on whether certain teams would then use the system or not. With little knowledge or experience of software development, stakeholders had little idea about the duration of tasks and so submitted requests, thinking that it was 'only a five minute job'. This kind of stakeholder intervention continued throughout the project.

Table 5.2   Case study analysis: Widening project scope

Appropriate models	Notes
Psychological profiling	A simple analysis of the stakeholders could be made to understand what their motivations are for being involved in the project using Maslow's model. This could then help to identify whether there are other ways that their needs could be met whilst reducing any negative impacts on the project.
Influence	One of the issues is around managing the change request process. Only soft influence methods are being used like communication and engagement. It may be that hard methods of influence need to be introduced such as an application and approval process that would effectively put a gatekeeper between those requesting changes and those that have to make them.
Behaviour	If the reason that so many stakeholders wish to be involved is simply to raise their profile, then you may be able to offer them this outcome without them having to impact the delivery of the project itself. An example of giving good exposure to these individuals would be to arrange meetings that can also be used to update them on the project.

	It is clear that the stakeholders making the requests are not the ones necessarily affected by their decisions (no moral hazard). This could simply be because they will not actually be held responsible for the failure or late delivery of the solution. It may also be that they are unlikely to be around in the same role during implementation. The end users will be the ones impacted and so it may help to give them a bigger role in the decision making.
Communication	In addition to introducing hard influence processes to manage the change requests, communication of clear cut-off points for any changes could be made. A method such as NLP could be used to formulate a communication strategy in order to achieve the desired outcome.

In the case study described, a change management process was introduced to the project. When a stakeholder made a request, a change request form was completed. This was a simple one-page document that outlined the request, an estimate of task duration, cost and also the impact on the overall project delivery. This was then sent back to the proposer for review and the project sponsor for budget approval. In this way, the consequences of the requests being made could be diplomatically and factually communicated. As soon as this process was established, stakeholders became more considerate about their requests. They finally understood that they needed expert input on the implications of the potential requests. Consequently, a reduction in off-hand requests was observed and project delivery became manageable. Superficial change requests that added little overall value but had a considerable cost disappeared entirely.

This process was successful because issues were dealt with equitably and transparently and everybody was making decisions based on the same information. This made the project easier to manage and deliver, since expectations were better handled. This is a good example of how the introduction of a simple process using hard power yielded excellent results.

Since many individuals were involved at the start of the project, each wanted to make their contribution noticed. When the contributions were in conflict with others, then high level diplomacy would be required to reach a resolution. In some cases, individuals will have become involved in the evaluation stage of the project simply because they want to be seen to be involved. Many projects are very top heavy at this early stage, with everyone offering contributions to the design of the project. The problems associated with this project stage can also be viewed as networking tactics. At the beginning of projects, many senior people are involved, potentially from various departments or businesses. In fact, were it not for the project, they may never have had an opportunity to meet. The start of a project is an excellent networking event. You will have the opportunity to meet high level influential people, find out what they are like and whether there is any additional benefit to be gained from such a relationship.

There are a number of other approaches that could be tried to manage the large number of stakeholders. For example, a gatekeeper could be put in place that collected the requirements from the various stakeholders and also ensured that the same stakeholders did not have direct access to the software implementers. This would mean that the stakeholders making requests did not feel ignored and also that the software implementers were not overwhelmed with ill defined requests. Another approach to deal with stakeholders diplomatically would be to create specific events where their input was sought and which also allowed them to network. The direct impact on the project deliverables could then be controlled more easily.

Redirecting the Project

EVALUATING OPTIONS

Sometimes the time allocated for project option evaluation may be short, making it difficult to research solutions thoroughly. Ideally, you need to make decisions based on having identified all of the important constraints. However, in practice it is rarely the case that there is sufficient time to research all options rigorously. There is a trade off when you push for the evaluation stage to be short. It is possible that potentially show stopping issues may not have been identified or that previously unidentified constraints emerge. For this reason, it might not be until well into project implementation that the problem is discovered. This is because once implementation starts, the focus is then on delivery rather than checking that the option evaluation stage was completed appropriately.

If an issue occurs that means a major change in direction is required, you will then need to decide how to manage it. Some project managers ignore problems and hope that they disappear given time. Others will be too swift to change the project direction without again giving it proper consideration. Whatever your management style, managing and communicating major issues and possible solutions is difficult. Being able to deal successfully with these situations will demonstrate that you are a strong leader.

CASE STUDY: PROPOSING MAJOR PROJECT CHANGE

Key project stakeholders wished to implement software with a well-known brand. However, once the project started, detailed research of the product revealed that it could not deliver the requirements. Although the official product specification was in line with the requirements, it was clear that it was not actually fully functional. It was in the early stages of development and as such it was inappropriate to deliver what was required for the project.

Table 5.3   Case study analysis: Proposing major project change

Appropriate models	Notes
Psychological profiling	The project manager could use an understanding of the motivations of the project sponsor to help formulate the best way to approach the communication of this issue. In addition, rather than taking a problem to the sponsor, the project manager could spend time researching potential software solutions to present as options for moving forward.
Influence	The project manager could apply soft influence to help engagement with the project sponsor, for example, demonstrating that others, like the end users, were also in accord with this need for change.
Behaviour	Project teams can be left in a difficult situation, when there is no moral hazard for the decision makers. Costly decisions should be considered during the risk management process early on. The project manager should ensure that problems like vendor lock-in are not an issue with any legacy systems.
Communication	The NLP approach of communication could be used to formulate a strategy for communicating the news. For example, a clear identification of the problems, potential solutions and a recommended strategy to move forward with the advantages and disadvantages all weighed up will make it easier for the project sponsor to make the change. This is really important since this is the desired outcome for the project manager.

In some cases the project board may have their heart set on a solution. Once the project team is in place and implementation starts, it may become apparent that the solution the project board wished to follow doesn't make sense. Somehow, you need to put forward your case and try to get a more suitable solution accepted. This can be a complex situation to manage and requires diplomacy and effective communication.

Careful consideration is required for communicating a change of solution to key stakeholders. Some of the findings from neuro-linguistic programming or transactional analysis can be useful in helping plan how to achieve this. You need to be focused on the objective and communicate with and influence people effectively, particularly in a situation where it may be difficult to reach consensus. A whole variety of influencing techniques may be required to manoeuvre the project in a direction that gives it a greater chance to succeed.

In the example given, there was pressure to adopt a software solution that did not fit simply because it had a good brand. In fact, the brand seemed more important than the actual product's capability. Finding solutions takes time and research, otherwise you risk basing decisions on impromptu suggestions. One consideration, especially if your project delivery is dependent on a particular niche vendor, is to have an appreciation of the scenario where the vendor is no longer available or needs to be changed. Often, when decisions are made for using a particular product or service provider, the practical implications of any future changes are not fully considered. The problems associated with vendor lock-in should always be included during the risk identification and management part of the project. The selection of software solutions can be used to illustrate some of the issues:

- Vendor unavailability: being left with an unsupported solution,

- Vendor change: deciding that other software is better suited to your project, and

- Vendor lock-in: restricting your ability to exit from any service agreements.

Some solutions will inevitably mean that you may become dependent on a particular supplier. Generally, the more specialized or customized the product you buy, the greater the dependency. Sometimes the work involved in moving to a different supplier with a cheaper solution may work out more expensive due to the migration costs. Right from the outset of a project, you need to be clear about what your exit strategy will be in case you do need to go down that route, particularly if the decision makers will be unaffected by the decisions that they make.

When there is a push to speed through the option evaluation and selection phase of a project, then it makes sense to perform a risk assessment, even if a light touch only process is used. This can identify where the gaps are in the evaluation process that has been performed and create an opportunity for discussion around the risks to the project if certain gaps are not explored further. In any case, this process would ensure that good process was being followed and that as the project manager you were raising the risks and issues as you best understood them at the time. If the project steering committee then decides to go straight into project implementation, then at least they will have been made aware of the potential problems that might occur. It will also make it easier for these problems to be picked up earlier if they occur.

RISKING A NEW SUPPLIER

At some point during the project, you may need to buy in a product or services. As any sales and marketing person will know, people buy from people they know and trust. If you want the people making purchasing decisions to be more open about choosing suppliers, then you will need to give this task to those people with the appropriate characteristics. Purchasing something different or from a different supplier always carries a risk. Many individuals would not be willing to take what would be perceived to them personally to be an unnecessary risk because they gain nothing from it personally. Instead the negotiations could go sour and they could get blamed, and in any case, it is far more effort for them to establish a relationship with a new supplier. Remember that there is comfort and security in not changing your way of working, as described by Maslow's safety and security level. There are other reasons that people could continue working with the same supplier.

- Trying to keep a relationship in place with a personally preferred supplier,

- Avoiding the extra work required in doing more research,

- Disregarding how much it costs or how good it is, and

- Benefiting personally from the sale.

When buying products or services, where you aren't convinced by the motivations of the person making the decision, then you should openly challenge it but if you are unable to do that, then you should at least try to influence the small print in the contract to make sure that you get a good deal.

- Be careful about making purchases with extended contracts,

- Ensure that there is an exit strategy,

- Be aware of renewals and get-out clauses, and

- Remember to negotiate the contract.

CASE STUDY: CHANGING THE PROJECT MANAGER TO ENABLE
SUPPLIER CHANGES

On one project, there was a situation where the project was not progressing at
the required rate. The suppliers that were being used were unable to deliver
the required results and what they did deliver was of low quality. Despite this,
the project manager continued to extend their service contract. The project
sponsor attempted several methods of intervention to understand the source of
the problem. After repeated failures, the sponsor decided to change the project
manager.

The new project manager was not given any information on the previous
suppliers. Instead their task was to use a clean sheet approach to setting up new
relationships with suppliers that could deliver the required results. The outcome
was that the deliverables were produced on time and were of both very high
quality and very low cost.

Table 5.4   Case study analysis: Changing the project manager to enable
             supplier changes

Appropriate models	Notes
Psychological profiling	The motivations of the previous project manager are unclear from the fact that they continued to use poor suppliers despite the issues and despite the warning signals from the sponsor. The fact that the new project manager was able to quickly move the project forward so successfully suggests that there may have been issues with the previous project manager that remain to be resolved about their performance.
Influence	The project sponsor in this case was unable to exert any influence over the previous project manager to get them to try new suppliers or to come up with a new strategy for moving the project forward. In the end, the sponsor used the main influence that they had and that was to change the project manager completely. This may not always be possible. Other approaches could have been to communicate directly with the suppliers to establish the issues and to see whether any resolution could be achieved.
Behaviour	The previous project manager seems not to be focused on the project deliverables. It could be that they are completely focusing on their own career management in some way that is not visible to the sponsor. An example of this would be the possibility of the project manager wishing to join the supplier organization.
Communication	Transactional analysis could have been used to evaluate the quality of the communications between the sponsor and the previous project manager.

In the case study, the project sponsor had to take drastic measures to get the
project deliverables back on track. Sometimes it may not be possible to identify
the reasons for a person's behaviour and if your attempts to resolve a situation

through communication fail, then other methods have to be implemented. In this case it was to replace the project manager. To establish the reason for the project manager not wishing to change suppliers the project sponsor could:

- Discuss the issues with the project manager,

- Contact the suppliers directly to understand the reason for the delays,

- Renegotiate service level agreements,

- Re-tender the work inviting the current suppliers to also tender, and

- Put in place payment terms that are linked to performance and delivery quality.

The project sponsor could also have researched into why the project manager might be behaving in the way that they were by:

- Talking to their line manager,

- Discussing the issue with human resources,

- Identifying any potential training needs, and

- Analysing whether their project manager's skill set met the needs of their role.

There will be times when it is inevitable that a change needs to be made. Under these circumstances it would be wise to make the change in a way that reduces any detrimental effect to the project. In the case study, replacing the project manager and changing the suppliers had immediate and positive impact on the project. Often, new suppliers can surprise us with their desire to provide customer satisfaction to new clients. Incumbent suppliers on the other hand can become complacent about relationships that are already in place and make less effort to deliver. Shopping around for new suppliers should be part of due process. This provides assurances that the best value is being received from suppliers and also that new and better suppliers are not being overlooked.

Working With Key Stakeholders

STAKEHOLDER ASPIRATIONS

When you have a strong driver on the project, or multiple stakeholders showing a significant interest in the direction of the project, then it is worthwhile understanding their aspirations. If you understand the motivation behind their strong feelings and the sources of their influence on the project, you will be in a better position to work with them. It may be that they are trying to manage their careers in a particular way or that they are trying to build a relationship and network with certain people. It may even be that they are passionate about the project because they truly believe that it adds value. Or they are inspired by the technology associated with it. However you feel about their motivations, understanding them allows you to work more effectively with them.

Working directly with the project originator and champion can be helpful in understanding how best to deliver. Their enthusiasm for the project should be used to engage the organization, make people feel that their contribution is valued and that there is a compelling reason why they are being asked to do something. It is worth keeping an eye on whether the champion is planning to see the project through to the end or not. This may not be under their control but it may influence how you want to go about managing the project.

The person championing the project may have various motivations, for example: to improve their visibility through association with a high profile success, or because they have a personal stake in what the project is designed to deliver. They may even be assessed on their performance on this project as part of their performance contract. In reality, there may well be a combination of all of these motivations at play. Awareness of people's ambitions and how they can affect decisions on the project is fundamental.

At this early stage in the project, the project sponsor and owner may be heavily involved, as will the management that is directly overseeing this activity. They will expect to intervene and have their say on defining the project to ensure that their requirements are met. If there are a large numbers of influential stakeholders, they may pull the project in many different ways, making the definition of the project vague and more difficult to finalize and deliver. At this stage of the project, it is interesting to see how different stakeholders behave. Some examples of stakeholder behaviour are given using the same situation as the 'Widening project scope' case study described earlier in this chapter.

CASE STUDY: STAKEHOLDER MOTIVATIONS

Stakeholder 1: Legacy system manager

This particular stakeholder was in charge of the legacy reporting system that was being replaced and was moving on to a different role. Consequently, even though he had the most relevant experience and knowledge to help the project address the previous system's issues most efficiently, his interest in the new project was minimal. The easiest course of action for this stakeholder was to interact as little as possible with the new team and to leave them to discover the issues on their own. In a small organization, the cost of this kind of lack of cooperation would be immediately apparent as there are not sufficient funds to repeat studies when an individual walks away with the knowledge and lessons learned.

Stakeholder 2: Outgoing project manager

The second stakeholder knew a lot about what would be required of the system at a high level, but had no experience of technical issues that could arise during the implementation. As a result, they volunteered a shopping list of items that they would like to be reported with little justification in terms of what would be done with the information or what resources would be required to deliver such information. People forget that it is not only the one-off cost of putting a new process or system in place. In the case of reporting systems there is also the additional ongoing cost of people entering data into the system on a weekly or monthly basis and of others having to make use of it, thus adding to what, in some organizations, is already a cumbersome role.

They were also interested in making a mark on the organization by implementing a system that was guaranteed long and consistent use because of the benefits that it promised. All parties would be using the same information and the same system for operating and managing the business. This stakeholder's desire for a system that would be widely used and over a long period was in tune with the needs of the organization.

Stakeholder 3: Incoming project manager

A new project manager was appointed mid-system implementation. The system had started off with a broad scope and large set of reporting requirements but was eventually whittled down to a very basic outline, even though much money and time had been spent putting the many system features in place. This made the system more manageable and less onerous on the reporting teams.

Table 5.5   Case study analysis: Stakeholder motivations

Appropriate models	Notes
Psychological profiling	When working with a large number of stakeholders and there are extremes of attitude towards the project, it can help to recognize their individual motivations (Maslow) as a way of making sense of their behaviour and to make it easier to predict how they might respond.
Influence	Engagement will normally need to be sought through soft influence techniques due to the political nature of the interactions to manage stakeholder expectations. You will need to establish whether you wish merely to achieve compliance through your engagement or need internalization. It may be possible to influence stakeholders through the use of centres of influences.
Behaviour	Understanding the possible effects their behaviour may have on their career may help. If stakeholders will not be held responsible for their decisions then there is a risk of no moral hazard. Belbin's model could be used to establish what the strengths and weaknesses of each of the stakeholders are. This could potentially explain their different approaches and attitudes towards the project.
Communication	The NLP approach could be used to formulate a strategy for communicating to the stakeholders. For example, a clear identification of the problems, potential solutions and a recommended strategy to move forward with the advantages and disadvantages all weighed up will make it easier to reach the desired outcome.

Stakeholder 1 is pursuing a simple career management tactic. There is nothing to be gained from them getting involved or providing detailed information. If he does share his knowledge, then it is likely that people will continue to return to him as an information source well into the future and perhaps as long as the system is live. By actively staying away from the project and avoiding any decision making, he ensures that he will not be called upon for this project again in the future. This is not necessarily the best course of action for the company but seems the best course of action for the individual concerned as it enables him to focus completely on his next project, without the worry of any baggage from this project that he is leaving behind. If engagement is essential with this stakeholder then the following could be attempted:

- Clearly state their role and make them part of the team,

- Identify the information required from them,

- Ensure that there is a benefit to them for remaining involved, and

- Include the delivery of certain tasks into their performance contract.

Stakeholder 2 was the first project manager and manifested a common career management tactic designed to raise their profile. If they were able to deliver a successful project, then this offered them a positive legacy to the long-term benefit of their career, in terms of promotion, influence over their next assignment, and likely involvement in more important aspects of the business. Leaving a legacy or being associated with a successful project has many benefits for the individuals involved. They will be able to carry the experience with them and their success will act as a badge of their competence, professionalism and ability to deliver, well into the future.

Maintaining a good relationship with the outgoing project manager can be important especially if they are a significant centre of influence. Even though they are actively managing their career, they may still be a valuable ally. You may even find it useful to seek their intervention on the project. Enthusiastic, driven individuals can help others become motivated. You need to make sure that the project does not suffer when they leave. You should put in place a suitable handover or change management process to ensure that no momentum on your project is lost. Or even that the original objectives of the project are not overlooked.

Stakeholder 2 is also someone involved in the decision making without needing to consider the consequences or provide any justification. They can ask for the objectives they want without any thought to the delivery, workload of the team or impact on the end users. Using anti-pattern terminology this is classed as *no moral hazard*. The large number of people required to input data into the system would not even be aware of the decisions that would affect them on an ongoing basis, long into the future. The implementation of the change management system eventually made it easier to deal with this stakeholder diplomatically. Another method would have been to add the delivery of their proposed tasks into their performance contract.

For Stakeholder 3, the issue was identifying the reason for this change. Project managers that join mid-implementation will often review the entire project and shape it to resemble something that they can believe in and implement. Some reasons for the changes could have been:

- Wishing to reduce personal workload,

- Receiving information from the end users that the system was too onerous,

- Avoiding conflict with end users, and

- Lacking belief in the value and benefits of the project.

The challenge was that the people who would eventually use the information for management were not involved in defining the objectives of the system. The incoming and outgoing project managers were required to make assumptions of what information they might wish to see. Later, the data for the management team was greatly reduced, because they simply did not have the time to see large detailed reports, and as it becomes apparent that the information in the system is used less, the value of the system is undermined. Those responsible for data input then started to question the value of their efforts. To resolve this, the management team responsible for using the reports needed to give a clear request that could not be changed at least in the short term, right from the outset.

In some cases, the information that has been requested in the past is no longer required. Static reports are often of little use in helping to run the business. In the case of a small business, the managing director is likely to have a handle on all of the costs and activities in the business. Thus they are able to make changes in any part of the activity relatively quickly, as they have good visibility of what is going on. However, in larger organizations the distance between the controller and the operational staff increases and this slows down the relaying of real time information to the management team.

INFLUENCING STAKEHOLDERS

There are differences between the official and actual project management processes simply because there are human elements and subtleties of interaction which overlay them. These interactions are not easy to define on paper or to be factored in to your project. Indeed, each person's perception of these same interactions will differ. More astute project members can accommodate these factors into their working style, decision making and influencing processes to a greater degree. There can be both direct and indirect methods of addressing the same issue and knowing which approach or combination of approaches would work best is crucial. To understand the politics that affect your project, you can start by understanding the intent of those involved and how they work, behave and think. Take a look at the following case study that describes a project team meeting.

CASE STUDY: SEEMINGLY SUCCESSFUL TEAM MEETING

So you have had a really successful meeting and everyone has come to an agreement on a plan, and tasks have been given owners who were present in the room. There was genuine enthusiasm about the project and great optimism about its successful delivery. You couldn't have asked for the meeting to have gone any smoother. Now that you are a week into the plan you are ready to follow up with all of the action owners to see how they are getting on with delivering their tasks. However, now that you are trying to get hold of people to catch up with them individually to check progress, you are finding it incredibly difficult to reach them. They are not responding to your email or phone communications. You have left several messages and are still waiting to hear back. You have decided to try to arrange face-to-face meetings instead and are finding that selecting any time that would be agreeable is proving impossible.

Table 5.6   Case study analysis: Seemingly successful team meeting

Appropriate models	Notes
Psychological profiling	Motivating reluctant stakeholders to work with you can be difficult. You will need to identify what it is that will make each stakeholder enthusiastic about being actively involved in the project. If methods of motivation are not immediately apparent, then you may need to engage them individually and directly to agree a way forward that is mutually acceptable.
Influence	For each stakeholder you will need to decide whether a soft or hard approach to influencing them is likely to succeed. In some cases, you may be able to refer the matter to their line manager to resolve. For more senior individuals you may need to attempt a more engaging style in order to encourage them to work with you.
Behaviour	The stakeholders could be behaving in this way due to some historical projects that have led them to switch off. It could be useful to identify the underlying causes for the majority of stakeholders to have behaved in this way. This information could then be used to explain why your project is different and why they should want to be more actively involved this time.
Communication	The TA approach of communication could be used create a communication forum that was adult and equally respected on both sides. Analysing the way that conversation panned out could help to identify the ego state from which the recipient was responding and perhaps whether they were being truthful.

The stakeholders were enthusiastic about the project implementation at the kick-off meeting, however when it came for them to deliver their agreed actions, they were non-respondent. Being enthusiastic and positive in front of senior management was an obvious ploy to appear not to outwardly disagree. Later they simply avoided the project team while focusing completely on their operational workload. Since the project team did not have any line responsibility over the individuals involved, it was difficult to get any meaningful dialogue going with them again.

Some eventually said that they had never agreed to any action, despite having clearly and openly approved it. They acted simply to keep senior stakeholders happy during the project meeting itself, because no one ever disagreed in public. What they said and what they did and what they 'remembered' that they had said would often be at odds with what had been agreed. This discrepancy created frustration, making it difficult to challenge stakeholders without inadvertently accusing them.

Some stakeholders decided that they would ignore the timescales of the project and wait to see if their tasks eventually disappeared or if the project team overlooked them. They were so used to being asked to deliver on projects that were never completed, they had learnt that if they waited long enough, then in all likelihood the project could come to an end or their specific tasks would no longer be required. This would then have saved them any needless effort.

This is an excellent example of where people have agreed to something and shown compliance so you may even feel that at the end of the meeting they have internalized your request, they really believe in the project and have great enthusiasm to get work under way. However, it is only later, which they may have intended or after further consideration, they have found that they are actually not that keen on being involved with your project. There are many ways of inadvertently showing dissent. Unfortunately, it is also a very difficult situation to manage as you may not have any authority over the resources that you need to work with. In this situation, all you have at your disposal is your ability to diplomatically influence people to work with you. Sometimes, this will mean that you will have to find ways to negotiate a better way of working with people. When you are working with people that you already know, then it can be easier to manage, as it may still happen, but then you have a better idea of when somebody means what they say and when they don't. If you observe carefully, they may tend to use the same sort of wording, terminology and phrasing when they mean something else and you can keep a look out for that. You also need to be aware of wider political issues that affect the team members as this will help you to anticipate any silent dissent in the team.

It can be frustrating working in an environment such as this. If you behave and act in a professional way, then you tend to expect others to do the same, in a sense expecting a complementary transaction using TA terminology. You may expect people to be honest and open about any objections so that they can be discussed and resolved. If they later challenge some point, then you expect them to initiate a dialogue to resolve the matter. You may believe that these suggestions would be common sense for everyone – but it is not always that straightforward. Some may feel that individually they cannot make a change or any impact and so are reticent about being honest and putting their neck on the line. This is especially true if their actions result in more work without any perceivable additional benefit, being far better to toe a positive company line and have a long and stable career. Clearly, the motivation of others is not always the same as your own. Some stakeholders in the case study were driven by a desire to:

- Reduce their visibility as a strategy for managing their workload,

- Maintain diplomacy by never disagreeing publicly,

- Keep busy with other activities, and

- Reduce the likelihood of any future involvement.

It is unusual for anyone to show and communicate outright that they are not interested in delivering the task or that they are being unhelpful. People have discovered that it is far easier to agree as that way it always looks helpful and friendly and then, after the event, you can be so busy with work that you don't have the time for follow up meetings. And since you had no intention of doing the work anyway, you can carry on as normal, comfortable in the knowledge that you haven't flustered the feathers of anyone that matters.

Failing your own ability to influence and resolve the situation, you may need to find other more creative ways to deal with the issue. You may, for example, find somebody else who can influence them, another stakeholder, their line manager or a friend. Or you could look at offering them something that is within your power in return for them completing an activity which you need them to. This can be both tangible and intangible. For example, you can offer them some help, some mentoring, or resources to help them with implementation. Or you could even offer them other methods of inspiration, for example, an opportunity to meet with someone who could be influential to their career or someone who could open doors for them which would otherwise be closed.

You could better try to understand their preferred way of working. Do they prefer to have face-to-face meetings or teleconferences? Do they prefer to come to visit you or do they hate travel and prefer for you to visit them? Do they prefer meetings at breakfast or lunch? Or do they prefer to run such meetings over a coffee? If you can be flexible with how you work with people and adapt to meet the way in which they feel most comfortable, then you may find influencing people a lot easier.

It will be important to avoid piling up the workload onto the few individuals that are genuine. Those seen to work hard and deliver will tend to be asked to do more and more, simply because they can be trusted. They will rarely enjoy extra financial reward but they will be loaded up with the work that others have failed to complete. This can end up having a negative impact on their motivation. If you keep giving more work to someone who is good while their peers seem to get off lightly, then you can create a situation where your star performers get de-motivated and eventually give up and leave.

THE ORGANIZATION CHART

The project charter is a useful document that lays out, sometimes at a high level and sometimes in detail, the overall objective of the project, who is involved, what the background to the project is and the roles and responsibilities of the team. Getting this document in place can itself raise a number of political issues.

One of the most political aspects of a project definition document is the organization chart. You should never be naïve about the power an organization chart can have, since it indicates the lines of decision making. The organization chart is often the element of the project charter that takes the longest to reach agreement on and you may find that several iterations over time will be required. If you are responsible for drawing up an organization chart, then be wary! If you inadvertently introduce ranking which is at odds with the operational organization structure, then this may cause some problems. Poorly conceived organization charts can act negatively by demotivating members. Putting together the organization chart will need to be a joint effort, with a process to involve and engage all parties. The case study overleaf looks at an example where the project hierarchy comes into conflict with the 'business-as-usual' hierarchy.

CASE STUDY: THE PROJECT ORGANIZATION CHART

A project organization chart was created which would cut across different teams in the organization. Operationally these teams were organized vertically, with little or no communication or work taking place across them. When the project organization chart was developed, a number of issues became apparent. From the project perspective, all teams would be impacted equally by the implementation. However, from the individual teams' perspective, they were not equal since the revenue generation in one team was far higher than in the others. The team leader for the high revenue generation team was organizationally a higher grade than his project counterparts. But on the project organization chart all team leaders were shown at the same level, since they represented the same linkages into the project office.

Table 5.7   Case study analysis: The project organization chart

Appropriate models	Notes
Psychological profiling	It is important to understand that the different team leaders will be at different levels in terms of their motivational needs (Maslow). A person's position in a company can directly affect their self esteem and confidence. If a person is shown to be lower than they believe they are, even on a project organization chart, then this can have a negative impact on their self esteem. For this reason, it would be wise to find some way of illustrating the difference if it means that this person will be more amenable.
Influence	Engagement will normally need to be sought through soft influence techniques due to the political nature of the interactions. A way in which this could be approached is to seek to develop the way that the organization chart is presented with the individual concerned. In this way, you could make them part of the process, take on board their comments and at the same time influence the direction of the end result.
Behaviour	Analysing their different ways of working (Belbin) may lead to suggestions on how best to work with the team leaders. It may be that if you are seen only to take input from the senior team leader, then that could cause resentment from the others. It may be more diplomatic to engage each of the team leaders individually to gather their input and create a version of the organization chart that has answered the most important issues raised in these meetings.
Communication	The TA approach of communication should be borne in mind when engaging each of the team leaders, particularly if one team leader sees himself above the others.

Since organization charts can be strong contributors to self esteem, this issue can be analysed using Maslow's theory of human motivation. Maslow described security and self esteem as important motivational factors. Both of these can be impacted through the organization, for example by:

- Relative ranking of individuals,

- Effects on promotions,

- Perceived worth and feeling of belonging, and

- Effects on ego and pride.

A person's job, how they perceive the value that they add to the organization, how they feel about working with other groups are all linked into self esteem. If we apply Maslow's theory of motivation, then you can see that it does matter to people how they are perceived in terms of their own self esteem and their feelings of job security. This is why you often hear people who are working for somebody else saying things such as, 'I have such and such a number of people working for me.' or 'I have my own administrative staff.' This all demonstrates how they judge their own value. If you take a step back, then you will see that anyone who works for someone else's business has nobody working for them, because they actually have no real power. Only the real employer or business owner does. Everybody else is an employee. If you are actually the owner of a business and you take the risk when you take on staff, then you are more likely to be aware that there is a big difference between the two. You may delegate some of your responsibility to others but at the end of the day you have the ultimate power to say who stays and who goes. Who gets hired and who does not. So the reality of power may not matter too much to people or they may wish to ignore it, but what does matter is their own perception of their value and ability to yield power.

You may face reluctance from stakeholders to get a project charter put in place and signed off. There are many possible reasons for this:

- Not ready to commit to some aspects in writing,

- Ambiguity is strategically more useful at that stage, and

- Delaying approval to create time for new stakeholders to join or leave.

Organization charts are seen as a direct, visible and concrete fact of your value and power lines that run through the organization. They can have a strong influence on staff motivation. An innocent mistake by a project manager can rapidly lead to conflict that is difficult to rectify. Even though it is understood that project organization is different to the operational organization, these conflicts occur because of the way positions are perceived. There is no way around this other than careful diplomacy in how you draw the project organization chart. Even if this means bringing teams together face to face to ensure that everyone is depicted in a way they are comfortable. Possible ways forward include:

- Collaborating with the team leads to develop the chart,

- Taking both project and organizational roles into account, and

- Clarifying responsibilities and interfaces.

6

Planning and Risk Management

Introduction

PROJECT DEVELOPMENT

Having completed a project charter, you can start defining how the project will be implemented in detail. During the planning phase, you can test whether the assumptions made during the project definition phase were correct and if higher level timescales agreed for delivery are achievable. It is also a good time to challenge the project definition and then build upon it. Important decisions will need to be made during this planning phase, such as resourcing, detailed budget allocation and identifying any risks and issues that will affect the project. Further information about planning can be found in Nokes and Kelly (2007), Posner and Applegarth (2008), Lock (2007) and Reiss (2007).

During the project definition phase and perhaps even during the planning phase, there can be a number of challenges to the successful completion of the project. Having a structured way in which to deal with these risks and issues as they arise will give people confidence in your management ability. The risk management process will ensure that all concerns are taken on board. Issues are the concerns or events that will definitely happen and that you will have to deal with at some point. Risks are events that may or may not happen and they will have a range of likelihoods and impacts that you need to consider. Risks and issues are mentioned here together because often these are raised together independent of whether they will definitely happen or there is a only chance that they may occur. Not all risks and issues will have the same impact and so when you plan the activities to manage them you will need to take that into account, particularly with respect to resource allocation. Obviously, it is better to focus on those which are the most likely to happen and will have the most impact unless they are effectively managed. Further information about risk management can be found in Kendrick (2009) and Chapman and Ward (2003).

RESOURCING THE PROJECT TEAM

Issues within the immediate project team may be an everyday consideration for you. Difficult situations can arise for a number of reasons and in a whole variety of ways. An effective combination of understanding motivation and behaviour as well as relationship management skills can help deal with these situations. It may be that on your project the hardest thing to manage is the internal project team politics. And since this is the group of people that you work with every single day, then it can be more important than ever to be diplomatic and sensitive about handling situations.

There can be politics between the team and the organization or even within the project team itself. In fact, it is more common for project team members to be stressed out by others on the team than anyone else they come into contact with. There will be people who have worked together and have got on and people that have worked together before and didn't get on. There will be people who were in superior roles in previous projects and now have less important roles compared to people they were previously managing. There could even be non-work relationships that could cause tensions. Various team members could be fighting to get their contribution openly recognized. Others will be trying to work their way through to more influential roles in the project as it progresses. Others could even be positioning themselves for their next project.

In an ideal world, you might try putting together a team using Belbin's team inventory model as a basis to ensure that you have all the 'right' types of people on your project team. In this way you may feel that you give your project the best chance of success. However, things rarely work out this way in practice and this does presuppose you know what a perfect project team might look like.

BALANCING PROJECT AND OPERATIONAL COMMITMENTS

One of the most difficult challenges that some project team members may face is the balancing act of day-to-day operational responsibilities with project activity. Project work can be a distraction from the critical activities that people with operational responsibilities perform in keeping the organization running. These ad hoc project activities can easily be a source of stress and frustration, particularly if there is much interest and pressure from senior management. There are some basic techniques that have been very effective with team members in these situations.

Dedicated resources can be easier to manage than shared resources, since you have a better idea of their work load and can manage their time directly. Once you start to share resources, it becomes more difficult for both the manager and also for the resource. They may often have conflicting tasks and timings or deadlines on both sides that coincide, making it difficult for them to keep either of the managers satisfied with their delivery. It is often not even possible for you to assess fairly how they are getting on and what they will and won't be able to do. This can be much worse if you never actually see them in person.

It is important to communicate clearly how much time any project activity will take and how much time you have available. This can help drive the discussion with management on ensuring precision in defining what project activities are crucial and exactly what outcome they desire. Agreeing a plan of action and a schedule further ensures that targets have been jointly agreed. This in turn can help to have the conversation around budgets and resource requirements. After a number of iterations of this process, a pragmatic plan should be achieved.

There may be tension between the dedicated resources on a project and those that are only involved part time. It may be difficult for dedicated resources to get time to see and work with the other team members. This can give them the sense of the other team members not pulling their weight and perhaps not giving sufficient time and importance to project activities. However, since you probably don't have any line management responsibility for those people, it can be difficult to judge whether they are putting in the effort that they should be or not. On the other hand, the individuals with split responsibility may find that they are being pulled in many directions at once and are finding it hard to prove to any party that they are doing a good job. There are many examples of where people have even taken advantage of the fact that they are working on several things as a tactical way of perhaps getting out of difficult meetings or having to complete difficult tasks.

A situation that arises from lack of time dedicated to a project by a team member who has other responsibilities is a very difficult situation for both the project manager and for the rest of the team to manage. Team members may feel frustrated and think they are being treated unfairly and it may be that this causes tensions within the team. As the project manager, you may have no way of really knowing how much effort and time is being put in on either your project or on other duties that the individual has.

This is an example where you need to use all the skills of judgement that you have to hand. You could apply what you know about that person and compare that to the needs analysis using Maslow's model and also perhaps do some personality and behavioural profiling using Myers-Briggs and the Belbin models. This will give you an indication of a person's motivational levers and also what their ways of working are. Using this information and your networking skills to talk to the other people involved with that person you can begin to understand how you might get the best out of someone who has such split responsibilities.

DEFINING THE CRITICAL PATH

This is an important, and often overlooked, part of the planning process. There needs to be a distinction between the 'must have' deliverables and the 'nice to have' deliverables on a project. Operational activities may threaten to impact the critical path and so you need to be clear on what action you should be taking when and if that occurs. Identifying and actively managing tasks on your critical path is a useful and underused tool. Often, tasks can get added to plans at the risk of impacting deliverables on the critical path. Defining the critical path can make it easier to prioritize key tasks. This is particularly useful when there is a risk of scope creep as the project progresses. Being able to clearly communicate the critical path also helps in engaging stakeholders and shows that you are in control of the important components of the project.

Managing the critical path is one of the project manager's key roles as this can ensure that the project stays on track. It also helps to resolve any conflicts there might be with operational activity. An ongoing review of the deliverables on the critical path can ensure that they are still valid and any risks can be flagged immediately to the project board.

DEALING WITH SCOPE CREEP

If there is no change management process in place then the scope of the project and resources can continue to increase. It should not then be surprising to be presented with an increased bill. Contractors and consultants can be directly incentivized to sell more work and they often do that by expanding your requirements to justify the extra resources. You need to ensure a transparent process is in place to manage proposed changes and that you have a clear indication of the costs involved. Often, decisions are not relayed to the project financial controller and this can also be a source of tension with suppliers.

Scope creep is a big challenge that a project team can face. The problem seems to get worse when more stakeholders are involved. This is an area where passive management can result in disaster since the scope of the project becomes so large that it is impossible to deliver.

Having a change management process can help this situation. However, scope creep normally requires you to diplomatically manage upwards and that can be difficult. Again, having an understanding of personality types and motivations may help you to come up with a better way of dealing with issues. One of the most successful ways to manage this kind of change request and scope creep is to put in place a simple process that needs approval before those changes can be implemented. This can act as sufficient deterrent for at least some of the problems associated with scope creep.

SUMMARY OF TOPICS

It is during the planning and risk management stage of the project that you may begin to engage with people that will actually be held responsible for the delivery and outcome of the project. Again, it is their strong engagement that is required for the project to be successful. A project manager must understand whether the person they are planning with will actually be executing the task or if they are simply responsible for their team to produce the deliverables. If the latter is the case, then even good buy-in with this level will not necessarily lead to a successful implementation. The topics considered in this chapter are outlined below.

Making plans:

- Planning for management visibility,

- Reluctant planners, and

- Providing structure.

Budgeting:

- Unrealistic budget, and

- Managing the budget.

Managing risks:

- Recording risks and issues,

- Facilitating risk reviews, and

- Categorizing risks.

Making Plans

PLANNING FOR MANAGEMENT VISIBILITY

It is not uncommon for there to be multiple versions of the same plan. This kind of dual planning can occur for many reasons. For example, one plan is used for the detailed delivery of the project and another plan is used for management reporting. Often these plans may have the same major milestones, but this is not always the case. Sometimes, management may be more interested in specific milestones only; for example, those that require management intervention. This can be a useful tactic, particularly if you have time constrained managers from whom you are trying to get meaningful input. Instead of drowning them in information, it can be better to focus their attention on where they can add value and then they should trust that the rest is all going to plan and is under your control. The political environment of the project will often dictate whether two sets of plans are needed or not. Some organizations have made a point of cutting back dual planning by only having the bottom-up plans as part of the performance management system. In this way there is no space for middle managers to mix up the message that is delivered to senior management through the plans.

Of course, there can be other reasons for not sharing your complete plan with others. Some people may wish to hide what they feel are personal proprietary methods of working or problem areas. They may use selected information to give a positive impression to an otherwise troublesome situation and hide the fact that there are problems building up in the pipeline. This can happen when they feel that it is an issue which is under their control and that they will be able to fix it by themselves, without recourse to others. This is a risky strategy, particularly if the problem continues to grow, making it increasingly difficult for that person to seek help. This situation occurs in many organizations and represents the kind of wishful thinking that can result in spectacular disasters.

Problems can gain momentum and size as time goes by; a problem may become compounded and hence far more difficult to resolve than if it had been properly addressed right from the beginning.

You don't necessarily need to be able to see all plans at all levels of detail. For example, you may give an estimate for some work to include some slack as contingency. That might be the plan that you share with your manager. However, you may have another plan which you believe is the more realistic plan that shows timescales when everything runs smoothly.

Certainly having multiple plans may be seen as duplication of effort and effectively a waste of resources. If you are keeping only a single plan then it may be worthwhile using wording and structures within the plan that meet the requirements of both sets of stakeholders, those that use it for management and those that use it for delivery. In this way, you can minimize the effort required in tracking the plan. The main deliverables could then be shown to management with the detailed tasks underneath available if they wish to see them.

CASE STUDY: IGNORING THE IMPLEMENTERS

A software developer was asked to provide timescales for delivering various programming milestones. The developer gave honest information based on what the timescales would be if everything went smoothly. The manager having collected this information then created a plan that was much shorter than that discussed with the developer. In effect, the manager disregarded the information supplied by the programmer and prepared a plan based on the timescales that he would like to have the milestones delivered by, in essence, taking no account of how the implementation would actually be done. This caused obvious frustration for the programmer when he found out, as well as the manager losing trust from his staff because of the way that he had behaved.

Table 6.1   Case study analysis: Ignoring the implementers

Appropriate models	Notes
Psychological profiling	It might be useful to understand what the motivations of the manager might have been in so obviously ignoring the information that was given to them.
Influence	It may be possible to put in formal planning processes that mean that the information prepared by the implementing staff is seen directly by senior management without any tampering by middle management. In this way, any potential problems cannot be as easily hidden.

Behaviour	It could be that the manager has not been completely honest with the programmer in communicating the customer requirements for the development work. There could be some political or tactical reason for the manager not to have taken the information from the programmer on board.
Communication	A study of the transactions between the programmer and the manager may reveal that they were not communicating from complementary ego states.

Here is a simple example of a developer being asked how long it would take to get a certain job done. The programmer gives an estimate of seven days and the product manager that was requesting this information adds this task to the plan and puts in a delivery time of two days. Obviously, the software developer then immediately feels that there was no value in the manager having asked for his input, as it was completely ignored. In addition, the manager then gave an estimate to the customer that was not agreed with the person delivering the task. There is a difference between when somebody might like to have the deliverable completed and when it is actually possible. This is an issue of who has the authority to dictate the terms of the planning process.

The manager wishing that the deliverable is completed earlier is all well and good but if he chooses to ignore the estimate that has been given to him by the person who will actually deliver the task then he has created an atmosphere of distrust. Second, the fact that the manager gave a false estimate to the customer without the developer's knowledge meant that he was seeking to override any authority or respect for the individual who has to deliver the task. How was that going to make for a good working relationship?

When a project starts and a plan is frozen, it is better for there to be some sort of guideline in place to ensure that only the right people can make changes to the plan. And there needs to be a clear process through which changes must go. Not all changes will have a direct impact on the project end date, as this can be monitored by creating and managing the tasks on the critical path well. However, increasing the workload of key resources can have an indirect effect on the schedule and also create an unnecessary atmosphere of mistrust and it is simply not a good way of working.

If changes to the baseline are allowed, then the project manager needs to be careful about what impact that will have on cost, resources and importantly what, if anything, needs to be fed through to the project sponsor. Some situations will be too small to highlight at that level and others will need to be communicated.

In the example, with the manager disregarding information given to him because he didn't like the sound of what he heard is not a good management technique. In particular, this is a really big problem when there are projects that have very real world tangible results, as is the case in construction, engineering and science projects. Either it works or it doesn't. Either it is built or it is not. There is no softer scale of measurement, where people can say that it is complete without there being any method of verification.

There are number of things that could have been handled better in the example given above. The main issue is of bad communication from the manager, where he did not seek to come to some kind of agreement or way forward with the developer. Instead, he chose to artificially impose his deadline regardless of how unachievable it was. This sets the software developer up for failure right from the start, since there was no expectation that the task could ever be completed in that time.

If you look at the communication that went on, you could see that it could have been clearly a case of a crossed transaction.

Product manager: 'I need this project done in two days.' (Parent to Child)

Software developer: 'This task will take at least seven days to deliver.' (Adult to Adult)

Each has made a statement in terms of what they think is necessary to get to the required outcome and yet since this has been a crossed transaction they have both gone away thinking that a different agreement has been reached. The manager has decided to ignore the developer and impose the two-day requirement on him anyway by then directly going to the customer.

Luckily, the developer understood what was happening and instead of accepting that indeed he was set up to fail on delivering in time for the deadline, he raised the issue with the customer who could then take it back to the manager and challenge him. Good managers will make sure that their team do not get bullied into something that is totally unachievable.

Once you are into the delivery stage of a project, you have to be very careful of scope creep. Where a project has been resourced and budgeted with a particular objective in mind you cannot let various stakeholders cram more into the project scope with an expectation that it will not impact the cost or the schedule. A good method of managing this is for all change requests to be made through and approved by the project manager. Then, for each change that is requested the project manager can put forward an assessment of the cost of the change, either in terms of resource time or money, and also the expected impact on the schedule. Once this assessment is made, it should then be signed off by the project sponsor so that it is clear that there is an impact for each change that is made. Almost always the people requesting an addition or change are unable to make a real assessment on the impact of their request. Unless of course they are planning to deliver those tasks themselves.

There are a number of potential courses of action that the programmer could take.

- Speak with the manager to understand the reason for the changes,

- Build in more contingency the next time plans are requested,

- Learn more about the customer requirements, and

- Bypass the manager when creating plans in the future.

As you can see, not all of these actions are positive. Managers who ignore their team can lead to their staff losing trust in them. In the long term, this can negatively impact working relationships. It is in the manager's interest to ensure that he does not make such mistakes through lack of proper adult communication. He needs to ensure that everyone understands the reasons for his actions.

RELUCTANT PLANNERS

When going through the planning process, it is worthwhile trying to get the key milestones and deliverables worded in a way that makes it clear to someone not intimately familiar with the project what is going on. Sometimes people will purposefully keep the milestones vague and ambiguous so that it is difficult to get a handle on what they are actually going to do and then to track how they are performing. This can be for various reasons. They might prefer to not give visibility to how they are working. Perhaps they know about certain issues and are not prepared to let others know. Not everyone will want to be managed by a project manager using project management techniques. This is especially true if an organization does not have a history or culture of using such management techniques. To some it can come across as overly bureaucratic and make people feel like you are stepping on their toes. They may challenge you by saying that they don't need to take part in the process at all.

As a project manager, sometimes these things are out of your control. But your responsibility is to raise the issue with the appropriate people and to do what you can to minimize these effects. Some team members will happily produce very detailed and lengthy plans and some may produce a list of only five milestones. You will have to judge the value of the content that they provide against what you are trying to achieve through the planning process. If the content of the plans is directly used for reporting purposes, then you will need to think about the wording of the deliverables and tasks used and how that rolls up into any high level plan. Sometimes the wording of milestones and deliverables may make sense to the owner but to no one else that uses the plan for other purposes. So you will need to form some agreement in the wording of tasks such that duplication of effort is avoided and the interests of all the parties involved in the process are served.

PROVIDING STRUCTURE

One of the main values that an experienced project manager can bring to the table is that of a structured way of breaking up the project into manageable chunks using some form of work breakdown structure. However, many project managers still use a long list of tasks to manage projects. Quite often as a project manager you may inherit a project plan that has pages and pages of tasks in no particular order with maybe some dates against them.

Many project managers do not have any formal training or qualifications and may never have come across some of the methodologies that are commonly used for project management. Typically, many senior and middle managers responsible for projects do not have any formal project management support behind them. That doesn't make them bad project managers. In fact, some of the best project managers are those who are not constrained by the knowledge of formal techniques. Instead, they have a vast amount of experience and this experience means that they know how to manage projects in the real world and to get things done. However, this is not always the case and untrained managers can struggle with the implementation of project management techniques.

CASE STUDY: PROBLEMS COMMUNICATING THE PLAN

Two joint project managers had been working together for several months and had put together what they considered a good plan but they were still having trouble communicating it to the relevant stakeholders and hence had issues with buy-in.

On looking at the plan it became fairly easy to see what the problem was. The plan had several pages of text, a brain dump of things that needed to be delivered. However, this plan didn't make much sense to anybody else since there was no structure or logical order to the information. Even though the content was basically good, the presentation of the information was poor and key activities were missed because they themselves found it difficult to identify the gaps.

Table 6.2   Case study analysis: Problems communicating the plan

Appropriate models	Notes
Psychological profiling	It could be useful for the project managers to establish each other's ways of working (Myers-Briggs) and to use that information to ensure that they take on complementary roles with clear responsibilities.
Influence	The project managers need to improve their ability to be seen as expert project managers. This would help them to engage with stakeholders more effectively. Some basic project management training could help in this case. Another option would be to have an experienced and trained project manager to come and advise them on how they could improve their planning and project management processes.
Behaviour	Both project managers could identify the strengths in their network and use that to help them to engage with their stakeholders. For example, through gaining advice on how they may best approach the stakeholders and which methods of communication and engagement work best with them.
Communication	Using both NLP and TA could be helpful in structuring a more successful way of communicating their plan.

A single list of a hundred activities is not necessarily the best way to communicate your ideas. Presenting planning information in a structured way will always make it easier to communicate to others. In this case above, the project managers hired a trained and experienced project manager to mentor them in order to improve their plan and also the project management processes that they needed to implement. This combination of in-house experts (who knew the business and had the relationships with the stakeholders) and an external project management expert who brought good process worked well. The project managers were able to harness the clarity that comes from clear structure and communication and were able quickly to engage and influence stakeholders effectively from then on.

SINGLE POINT OR SHARED ACCOUNTABILITY

When assigning tasks, it can be tempting to assign them across two different groups to encourage some form of joint accountability. Managing tasks that have joint ownership may be more difficult because this approach can obscure the contribution that each party makes. You need to make extra sure that the deliverables have been clearly defined and that everyone is clear about what success would look like. A combination of soft and hard power to influence and incentivize people to get things done will be required.

In many organizations from time to time there will be a swing from single point accountability to shared accountability. These two different approaches go in and out of fashion because there are advantages and disadvantages to both. Having shared accountability on tasks can sound wonderful, especially if you are trying to get two parties to work closely together to get something completed. However, in general, activities where there is a shared responsibility and accountability, can also be more difficult to achieve; neither party can take full control of the delivery of the task, and so it can be difficult to coordinate and ensure that things don't fall through the gap between the owners of the task. Shared accountability also makes it difficult to place responsibility when things go wrong and to get things rectified. It may also be used tactically as an excuse to get out of doing anything and indeed, when people don't share the workload of the task evenly, this may lead to feelings of unfairness. If it is unclear how the achievement of a shared task will benefit both owners and how and who will get the recognition for the work, it can be difficult to motivate people to get the task completed well.

It is easier to give people tasks that they are individually accountable for. Putting these into their individual performance contracts makes an even stronger case for ensuring that the tasks are properly executed. If people are not held accountable for their delivery on tasks, then there is often little other incentive for them to complete them. Unless of course, completing that task eases their workload in the long run or has some other beneficial side effect for them directly. Many project teams find dealing with this aspect of accountability very difficult because you cannot 'make' people do things and so you need to find other ways of getting to the same end result. You need to use all the softer skills that you have at your disposal.

Of course it depends on the people to whom you give shared accountability and the tasks they need to complete and the context within which all of this is set. Regardless of whether you set a task to be shared or single point accountability, you need to make sure that it is clearly understood and that what success would look like is clearly defined. You may need to incentivize people and to influence them perhaps using even a combination of soft and hard power. The consequences for not getting a task complete should also be made clear. If cooperation is needed, then it is best to find ways in which you can encourage and show the different groups the individual benefits they will see by working together effectively.

Budgeting

UNREALISTIC BUDGET

Sometimes it is obvious from the outset that the timescales involved in delivering a project are far too tight. If you are tendering your project or activity, then you need to establish realistic times for delivery and ensure that your suppliers are not simply telling you what you want to hear. If the proposal for completing the project sounds too good to be real, then it may well be. Expecting a cheaper supplier to do a better a job and deliver on time compared to a more expensive supplier being honest about what it is likely to take to complete the work may be wishful thinking.

There can be many tactics at play here. If a supplier is keen to get the work, then they may agree that everything that you ask for is indeed possible in the timescales and budget that you are looking for. Even if they know that it will either not be possible or a real struggle, they may plan to request an increase in resources and budget from you at a later date. At that later stage, it can be too late to change supplier, or certainly make it very difficult to do so. Even if you do not increase the end date or the resources to deliver the project later, you would risk ending up with a substandard delivery or a product which does not quite meet your requirements.

CASE STUDY: UNDERESTIMATING THE BUDGET

A project manager was approached to prepare a proposal to deliver a web-based software solution for managing membership information. Having gone through the request for proposal (RFP) documentation and assessed the target budget for the project, it was clear that it was not possible to deliver the product required within the budget available. Taking the approach of being the lowest cost supplier would inevitably mean that the product quality would be significantly compromised.

Table 6.3   Case study analysis: Underestimating the budget

Appropriate models	Notes
Psychological profiling	Studying the RFP documentation can give an insight into the working style of the client. If they have prepared a very detailed account then they are likely to want a detailed response. If however, they have only given an outline of the requirements and wish to leave the details to the supplier then a different type of proposal could be constructed (Myers-Briggs).
Influence	You could try soft influence methods in order to communicate the difficulties with the budget constraints.
Behaviour	The tight budget of the RFP could simply be a tactic by the client to see how much is possible and to push the suppliers on cost. It is a risky strategy given that bespoke development is required.
Communication	Since the goal of the response is to win the contract, it is possible to construct the proposal in such a way that it gives the customer options. You could prepare a proposal with what is realistically achievable in your opinion given the timescales and budget and also prepare some options that would enable the client to receive a quality product. This way you give yourself as many options for being accepted as possible.

As a project manager you need to be aware of unrealistic budgets and timescales. Clients and stakeholders will often push hard to get as much value in as short a time and as low a cost as possible. The most honest approach for the project manager would be to prepare a proposal with what is achievable given the timescales and then give options for additional work if required. In this way, the project manager is not setting up unmanageable expectations that may cause trouble if the proposal is accepted. When preparing a proposal under time pressure it can be easy to forget that there is often more than one answer to any proposal and there is no reason why suppliers cannot provide a range of options with a highlighted recommended option. Using the transactional analysis terminology, this provides the most adult response to the proposal.

There are other courses of action the project manager could take. For example, they could agree to deliver the full requirements within the budget made available. This could mean that they potentially take on the project at break even or even at a loss. Sometimes, this can be strategically important, particularly if you are trying to gain a new client or to gain experience in a new industry. Not all benefits are financial. This could then potentially lead to new contacts or more work that is actually profitable.

MANAGING THE BUDGET

In a small business, keeping costs down has an immediate and sometimes substantial effect on the people running the business. This is especially the case if earnings are directly related to profitability. However, this relationship becomes diluted the larger a company becomes, making it difficult to incentivize people to minimize costs. This is because an individual's contribution and effect on the organization is normally not clearly recognizable.

Larger organizations also tend to work to budgets. This can work artificially to create a situation where there are no incentives for minimizing cost. In fact, there are often penalties, such as reduced future budgets, for working below pre-set budgets. Therefore organizations can work towards meeting their budget exactly, even if this sometimes means that they could have completed the project for less. It is important to be aware of tactical uses of the budget and understand when that is occurring and when it is strategically beneficial to do so. Budgets can be used up in many ways through hiring more people or by purchasing equipment that is not necessarily immediately required.

Unless there is a clear reason to shop around for the best value then the easier option will always be to go with what you already know. Shopping around for services and products, especially business to business services, requires a particular skill set and perseverance. Research and good negotiation abilities can be critical in getting a good deal.

Take the simple example of getting some printing done for part of a training programme implementation. Ringing around companies for quotes and understanding the pricing structure can highlight ways in which to negotiate a better deal, either by larger quantities, changing materials or working to different timescales. It can also give insight into whether there are other companies that would be better suited to delivering your requirements. Speaking directly with suppliers can highlight what the strengths and weaknesses are in light of your requirements. Also, you may find out who they were planning to outsource your contract to if you had accepted their offer. In which case, you could consider contacting such companies directly.

Buying, selling and negotiating all require a certain skill set, an ability to ask the right questions and to structure the requirements in various ways so that you can arrive at various pricing models. Understanding what you are buying is often the first step into being able to successfully negotiate a better deal. Negotiating is hard work and finding, contacting and chasing suppliers for quotes is a time and energy consuming activity that not everybody is good at or enjoys. However, you can see that having a certain attitude towards spending, managing costs and putting in place simple processes may effectively reduce the cost of projects. However, if all you are required to do is to use up your budget, then there may not be any reason to make the extra effort to minimize your expenditure at all.

If you have to manage tightly within a budget or you need to buy in services or solutions, then you should ensure that you have the right people in charge of that area. There will be certain personality types who will be more suited to such a role than others. If researching requires ringing around, chasing people and quizzing people on their pricing structures, then you will need to try and use staff who are extroverts and are able to work without having lots of detail to help them move things along. You will need people that can pick up signals both verbal and non-verbal about what they can and cannot achieve in terms of pricing or structuring a deal.

Project managers can often be in a situation where they will be responsible for some form of purchasing or staffing decision, and so being aware of what kind of levers you could pull in order to get the biggest bang for your buck can really help to make you a successful project manager. In general, people running projects are not trained in sales, marketing and negotiating techniques and even if they have some training, they may not have the right experience to do the job that you have in mind for them. A combination of training and experience usually gives the best results.

Managing Risks

RECORDING RISKS AND ISSUES

Many risks and issues can be raised during the planning process. It can be easier to set aside a specific time to sit down with the team to focus on identifying risks and issues and then putting together tasks and owners into the plan that will work towards mitigating them. In this way, you can keep planning meetings focused. This is particularly true if these meetings are to involve a large group of people, as issues and concerns can be recorded and given the proper consideration and time that they deserve separately. The terms risk and issue are commonly confused. Issues are events that will happen and you know that with certainty and so you must plan in a way that takes that into account. Risks are events that might happen and may affect your project to varying degrees.

Some teams will have experience of how to manage risk and others may never have come across such activity before. Deciding how to manage risks and issues can also raise problems. Some people may feel there is little value to be gained from such a process, if they have gone through a risk management process before. Or it could be the opposite, where they wish to implement a very detailed risk management that is not suited to the nature of the project.

The key in implementing a risk management approach is to ensure that it is done using the appropriate level of rigour and analysis that the project warrants. An onerous process that is detailed but that no one will use can be of little value. So it needs to be appropriately practical and managed in a way that is seen to add value to the project delivery.

CASE STUDY: BYPASSING THE INTERNAL RISK MANAGEMENT PROCESS

On one project, the manager knew that they had access to the internal risk management team to come along and carry out the firm's standard risk management process. However, they decided that having them in would mean that a detailed and numerically analytical risk process would be performed that would leave him with a big report. The manager felt that it would tick all the right boxes, but that he would still not realize any practical value from the process.

So he decided to use a more practical approach to risk management, where a short meeting, no longer than two hours, with no more than six people was arranged. This meeting was to achieve only two things: identify the risks and issues and attach owners to them.

After this meeting, each owner was met with to categorize the risk (importance, probability and impact) and come up with mitigating actions that could be tracked in a plan. The project manager then pulled all of this information together and distributed it to the team and arranged a follow up meeting where people could challenge the categorization or proposed actions.

Table 6.4   Case study analysis: Bypassing the internal risk management process

Appropriate models	Notes
Psychological profiling	The fact that the project manager chose to avoid internal processes shows something about the way in which he prefers to work. Bearing this in mind should help future engagement.
Influence/Behaviour	The project manager in this case did not succumb to the organizational pressure to conform. This indicates that he is likely to be an independent thinker and pragmatic in his approach.
Communication	The project manager should probably still involve the internal risk management team in some way, so as to not alienate them and potentially create future problems.

This is a good example of where the project manager decided he preferred to do things a different way so that he could get some practical value out of the risk management process. This method meant that he and his team spent less time doing the risk process but what time they did spend was focused and effective. So that instead of coming out the other end with a detailed report that no one would ever read, they came up with practical implementable actions that they could use to mitigate the risks that they were most concerned with. The key to running such a risk workshop successfully was to ensure that the right people were in the room, or at least were represented in the room so that all aspects of the risk profile of the project could be addressed.

An important aspect of managing risk is to ensure that all aspects of the project's risk profile are considered. The scope of the risk to the project should include:

- The political environment, both internally and externally,

- The reliance upon suppliers, customer or users, and

- The events outside of normal control, for example, health and safety.

Sometimes individuals can become fixated on risks that can seem really unrelated to the project or be so unlikely that they are not even worth considering. On the other hand, you do need to cover all of the relevant aspects of risk. This can be managed by having representation from all the appropriate groups during the risk identification process. It can also help to bring in external help from someone who understands the context and can bring objectiveness to the process. They may spot problems that maybe others deeply involved with the project would have overlooked or have been too narrowly focused to have noticed. It is good due process to document and manage risks and then to review them on a regular basis, including their categorization if appropriate, to see whether they are still risks or whether they have increased in likelihood or possible impact on the project. Sometimes even basic risks like system failures or power outages are overlooked and these could have significant impact on deadlines or the ability to deliver. On some projects, even the weather can be a critical factor. Having a 360 degree risk approach should help to minimize missing potential problems.

One of the most worrying mistakes to make during the scoping of the risk assessment is to miss out a category of risk altogether, for example, not to address important areas like health and safety or the dependence on particular staff to get the job done. During the risk process, it is important that people's thinking is not rail-roaded into looking at a certain area or a certain group of areas. Managing risk meetings is notoriously difficult and it is important to get someone appropriate to manage and facilitate the process, particularly if you have representatives that are high level managers and they are really focused on their area at the expense of others. You need a strong facilitator for these meetings to ensure that they run smoothly, that they get value out of every single attendee who was present so that no one feels that it was a waste of their time. Remember, they are all there representing some area and they need to be heard. So if you have a room full of different personality types, as the facilitator you will need to involve them and engage them in a way that works best for them.

Additionally, having an idea of the personality types of the people involved will help you to design a risk process that is most suited to delivering the best value for the team. If, using Myers-Briggs terminology, you have introverted personalities involved then they may not be able to provide the information that you need from them in a short meeting. They may need the time to go away and digest the information before they are able to make their value added contribution. You need to make sure that everyone's input is collected and to work with them in the way that best suits their personality type.

FACILITATING RISK REVIEWS

If risk management meetings are kicked off with a brainstorming session, then you can quickly be flooded with items as the facilitator. This is of course better than nobody having anything to say at all. But if people raise issues and then the team starts discussing how to resolve them and how bad the impact could be, then you could end up talking about one risk alone for several hours. The problem with running a workshop like that is that you may then not have time to collect everybody's feedback on other risks and they may also run out of energy to give you that information. You may even end up spending a lot of time on risks that are really unlikely or, even if they did occur, they would have little impact and then not have much time left over to spend on risks that were both more likely and would have a greater impact on the project.

It is really important to facilitate these meetings well and if you don't think that you have the skills or the experience to run them, then getting someone else in who can is sensible. This way you can save a lot of time and frustration in the process and end up with more meaningful results and a happier team.

CASE STUDY: RISK BRAINSTORMING SESSION

There was one such risk brainstorming session that was carried out with about 20 people. With so many people in the room, it was going to be difficult to facilitate the meeting in a way that added the most value. This was both in terms of output from the meeting and also from ensuring that the best use of the resources was made. After all, you were effectively spending 20 days' worth of resources as they were stuck in that room for the entire day doing this risk workshop. As a project manager, you should not forget that there is a cost to having these resources sitting in such meetings and that it may not be the best use of their time or the best way to get their input.

Table 6.5   Case study analysis: Risk brainstorming session

Appropriate models	Notes
Psychological profiling	It would be good to understand the motivations of the organizer of the meeting for insisting on so many people being present.
Influence	Perhaps certain stakeholders have been invited to exert influence over others.
Behaviour	Design by committee and group think could be potential problems here.
Communication	The facilitator will need to provide clear goals for the meeting and keep the discussion focused and on track.

It transpired that the presence of so many people was due to the fact that some of them did not want to feel left out of the process. They believed that if they didn't need to be in this meeting, then how many other meetings would they be left out of in the future. So, for some individuals, it was a matter of being present in the right company and in the right meetings. For others, it was a way of getting out of doing something else or of getting visibility in front of other influential individuals. There are many reasons that such meetings can inflate into an unmanageable size and as a project manager it would be your responsibility to have some kind of understanding of that so that you can still get what you need out of the meeting to manage the project risks going forward.

This design by committee approach meant that progress was slow and there still needed to be quite a lot of one-to-one follow up after the meeting. It would have been better to have a shorter meeting, perhaps even with a smaller number of people and then to focus on highlighting concerns and risk owners. Outside the meeting, the project manager or risk manager could collect the information they had so far, and then follow up with individual owners to collect their mitigation actions and timescales for delivery. Once that was all collected they could distribute that material and arrange meetings with other stakeholders to collect their feedback. Then if appropriate they could arrange a short follow up meeting with everybody together to present the results, show that the mitigating actions had been added to the overall plans and then finally to collect any remaining feedback before signing off the risk management activities baseline ready for implementation.

Big meetings or workshops tend to be frustrating for most people involved. Unless they are focusing on one-way communication and information sharing, you really have to question the value of them. It may feel nice for you to organize a meeting with so many high level people and feel that they are involved, but you won't really be able to get much individual value out of them being there.

A combination of the two types of meetings tends to work quite well. You can use the short, large meetings to observe any political issues between stakeholders and share information. However, one-to-one meetings will help you to get more value and also reduce the effects of group think and design by committee. You are also more likely to get honest information in smaller meetings as there will be far less peer pressure involved.

CATEGORIZING RISKS

Sometimes people can get distracted by risks that would not have a significant impact on the project and it can be difficult to move the discussion on from there. It is really important to ensure that the likelihood of the risk is also understood. Otherwise, more pertinent risks may be left without being discussed sufficiently. Focusing on and clarifying the likelihood and impact of potential risks and issues can help put them into perspective. Sometimes people may simply be passionate about an item or particularly concerned about it but you cannot let them dominate meetings and discussions at the expense of others not having a say or some avenues of risks and issues not being explored.

The likelihood and impact of risks can change with time and also the appropriate level of mitigating risks that are attached to them. Risks need to be regularly reviewed and followed up on. It is all too often that risks workshops are full of enthusiasm and passion and then when it comes to actually implementing the actions there is little evidence to show that any progress has been made on the mitigating actions.

CASE STUDY: RE-EVALUATING RISKS

There was much enthusiasm and discussion about all that could go wrong on the project and debate over what should be done. Team members were forthcoming in putting themselves forward as owners for delivering the risk mitigating actions. However, when it came to deliver, the same individuals were not taking the tasks as seriously as they first did in the identification and development phases.

Continual chasing of the owners revealed that no progress had been made on the tasks. Since that was the case, a review of all the risks and issues and their categorizations was performed again and it was found that many of them began to be downgraded in terms of their likelihood and their impact. And where they were more likely and had bigger impacts, it was decided that actually there wasn't anything that could be done about them after all. The outcome was that for one reason or another there was no need for many of the actions originally and studiously put together to be carried out at all. The risks were no longer as important as they used to be.

Table 6.6   Case study analysis: Re-evaluating risks

Appropriate models	Notes
Psychological profiling	It would be good to understand if there have been significant changes to the motivations of the risk owners that could be impacting their attitude.
Influence	If serious risks are being ignored then it may be necessary to find ways to exert influence to still get the mitigating actions completed.
Behaviour	There could be some tactical play involved here in order to minimize workloads.
Communication	Ensure that the communication level of the project manager stays adult and that he tries to keep transactions complementary.

Often at the start of the project, many people raise objections and concerns and sometimes these can be completely off the mark in terms of the impact and likelihood. It's only that at the beginning of a project, there are so many uncertainties and worries it can make people feel insecure; a fear of the unknown. And as you can see from the Maslow model, changes and making people work outside their comfort zones can create that kind of concern. The very nature of projects is such that they are often once off activities with no prior knowledge that they can associate with.

That is not to say that these concerns are not genuine. In most cases, they certainly are. Sometimes they are raised for political or tactical reasons as a way of raising some other issue or raising the profile of some other concern. But often it is a genuine unknown that causes the raising of risks and issues. This is again an example of where you need to be aware of personality types and people that are prone to anxiety. You need to be able to think about how you will get the best out of people and ensure that you get from them the value added information that they have. You then need to work with them to influence them and remind them of their initial enthusiasm when it comes to implementing the risk mitigating actions.

You need to be aware if there are cultural issues that need to be taken into account, as this can affect people's attitudes and awareness of risks. It can also determine whether they have a culture of taking risk seriously and doing something about it or whether they have a culture of being far more reactive to situations. Being in a reactive culture will mean that they won't do anything until they absolutely must and that way they only focus on what they know for certain. More pre-emptive and proactive work cultures will be more active at managing their approach to risk and will look at ways to minimize it.

7

Implementation

Introduction

DELIVERING THE PLANS

Once you have plans in place, it is time to start implementing them. At this stage in the project, tracking against the plans and reporting progress is critical to ensure that any potential show stoppers are identified early and timely intervention can take place. Key factors also include having the right resources and making sure that they work towards the same objective. A project manager must not only track plans, they should also be aware of political issues that are either present or that may present themselves in the future and shoulder responsibility for taking decisive action to get through as best as possible to deliver a successful project.

Inevitably, there will be matters that you discover or better understand as the project unfolds. Taking these continual changes into account, you must steer the project and the team to stay on track to deliver. You will need to be in control of managing changes to the baseline and ensuring access to the appropriate people and information. In addition, you will need to ensure that the information that you have is detailed and accurate enough for you either to intervene yourself or to seek management intervention when activities are not proceeding to plan or when critical risks and issues present themselves. Part of this will rely on your ability to seek help from others when appropriate and without feeling that it is a failure on your part. This will mean that sometimes you will need to be the messenger of bad as well as good news. How you manage this interface and deal with issues as they arise may be a key factor in your success as a project manager and the success of the project itself. Identifying ways to be proactive and responsible in your management of both small and large, internal and external, risks and issues will all be important.

If planning was initially done without any operational input, then this may be urgently required to highlight any necessary changes and to put in place access to the correct individuals responsible for delivery. Since performance management and reporting are the key activities of the project manager in this phase of the project, it is important that the correct individuals input into the reports and that issues are quickly elevated for resolution to the appropriate people. Further information about implementation, tracking and reporting can be found in Nokes and Kelly (2007), Posner and Applegarth (2008), Lock (2007) and Reiss (2007).

KNOWING WHEN TO USE EXPERT RESOURCES

Identifying when you need to bring in expert resources is a skill in itself. Not everybody will be able to make these observations and decisions. You will need to be careful about who is given the responsibility of making such decisions, particularly if budget management is a really important factor.

At different stages of a project, it can make sense to have different team compositions. In a small business, you would achieve this through bringing in expert contractors to deliver specific parts of the project. This is also the case in larger organizations where consultants, accountants and lawyers are brought in to perform specific functions. For example, at the beginning of a project you may wish to explore creative and innovative ideas on how to proceed and so you may bring in a blue sky consultancy. As you move into getting down to the details of the project, you may wish to bring in a consultancy that specializes in managing project implementations alongside business-as-usual activity. For both the technical and the legal parts of the project you may wish to bring in external experts in these areas. This approach to running your project can ensure that you get the most appropriate support for the various parts of the project. Sometimes trying to get one firm to supply all of your needs is simply not optimal.

Pulling other members of the client organization onto the project team can be just as difficult. It may not always be possible to pull in the best people to get a job done and sometimes you have to make do with the support already in place. This is often the case with small businesses where a few people are responsible for a wide range of activities.

Identifying, sourcing and managing expert resource requirements are key skills. Not everybody can do this effectively, and not everybody will be as aware of a project's needs as others. If you are the project manager, then you will want to make the best use of the resources that you have and also ensure that when you do bring on expert resources, that they are the correct people for the job that needs to be done. Using models such as Belbin can be a starting point for identifying the right resources.

UTILIZING NETWORKS

It may take time to get an official project organization chart in place. However, as time goes on you can find that there are better ways of getting things done that don't necessarily follow the official lines of the organization. This situation can arise for a number of reasons. Some of the people on the project may have worked with others previously and have a relationship beyond that illustrated on the organization chart. Try not to feel frustrated about the fact that this is how the real world works. Instead, learn to observe and make use of these situations and be politically astute enough to ensure that you sensitively manage issues that are handled using unofficial channels. You may already know of people who are excellent at using their network to help them move their work along. There is no reason that you cannot learn to do the same. You need to be able to:

- Identify the official and unofficial structures,

- Recognize the real decision makers and gatekeepers,

- Use your own relationships to get things done, and

- Identify and network with centres of influence on your project.

If there is a virtual organization of which you are unaware, then you may feel frustrated when you are performing your tasks and seeking the appropriate permissions and yet little seems to result from your efforts. This unofficial organization can exist if there are underlying structures that have developed. These can occur under all sorts of circumstances, like specific networking and training events, and are often positively encouraged in some organizations. This development of two distinct project teams can occur for a variety of reasons.

1.   Some of the individuals have worked together before and so there are alternative relationships that may provide shortcuts (or indeed be an obstacle to effective working, if their experiences have been negative).

2.   Informal networks may exist. This can be simply because they share common interests, or they like to go for a coffee or for a smoke. Sometimes, these shared interests can cut across organizational structures in terms of building personal networks.

3.   You may find that you get along with and understand certain people better than others and because of this you are more likely to search them out first rather than follow the official lines of reporting and responsibility.

You may initially start off following the processes set down by the project organization chart, however with time you may find better ways of working. The project organization chart is a great starting point and it also is the official way of doing things and so you must be sensitive to any issues that may arise if you bypass official channels. It is important to be self-aware in this process; there may be times where you are tempted to use an informal route to get a quick result, when in fact it is important not to undermine the project or people within it by excluding someone simply because you find it easier to work with another colleague. Using your informal project structure or following the official structure is always a matter of judgement.

You will need to develop and understand underlying relationships that are at work beneath the official chart. Once you realize that other relationships are at play, you can then start to think about how you can use them to your advantage. This use and development of your networking skills can play a major part in your success in the workplace.

KEEPING HOLD OF GOOD TEAM MEMBERS

You may be lucky enough to have a star performer or a great centre of influence on your project. They can be great assets to a project. They can motivate teams by the fact that they are involved. Misuse them or ignore them at your peril.

Some people will want to steer clear of certain projects if they feel that they don't further their career. Particularly if these projects have a high risk of actual failure or even of being perceived as a failure. For this reason, it can be difficult to get even worthwhile projects appropriately staffed. Tough projects that have desirable outcomes will either attract or deter the best candidates. Those who need to show that they can do this kind of work will be attracted as they have something to prove and something to gain. Others will be deterred from joining since they may feel that they no longer need to prove that they can run this kind of project. It doesn't gain them any additional benefits and so why should they take on a project which is going to be stressful with no additional bonus or advatage.

Organizations can be effective at identifying superstars and then relying on them over and over again to get things done. However they won't pay them any extra and still expect them to not burn out even though they are worked much harder than everyone else for no extra benefit to themselves. These superstars get a reputation for being able to get tough projects done and in fact their reputation becomes a burden since they are worked hard until they begin to suffer.

If you are in the lucky position of having such an individual on your project team, then they can certainly help to get the project moving as well as acting as an excellent motivator for the rest of the team. On the whole, superstars want to have their efforts acknowledged. In practice, the opposite tends to happen where they are overworked and under-appreciated. Treat your superstars unjustly and if they are smart, they will figure out what is going on and get out!

ESTABLISHING THE POLITICS

It is not always possible to be aware of the issues on a project until you join. However, you can make the greatest influence on a project right at the start. Later, once you are settled in, it can be far more difficult to make any changes. It may seem like a lot of extra effort, but finding out as much as you can about the project, the people involved and any issues that are currently troubling them will mean that you will be joining well informed and ready to take advantage of your entry onto the project. Your skills at gathering information and making an assessment of the situation and adapting your style and behaviour accordingly will help you in the long term to reduce any stress on the project.

If you are joining from outside the parent organization onto a team whose members have all worked together before (for example, a subcontractor, consultant, accountant or lawyer) then making sense of the prevailing politics will be harder. You won't have the same starting point or frame of reference as everyone else. You may be coming from a different company, department or expertise – any of these can make it more difficult for you than everybody else on the project to get to grips with the politics involved.

On the other hand, you can make use of the fact that you are an outsider, and won't necessarily need to be bound by the same unspoken boundaries that everyone else obeys. For example, project team members may feel anxious about speaking to certain people directly. However, you may not have the same inhibitions to stop you from approaching those same individuals. As an outsider, you may get away with bypassing these unwritten rules, but you'll need to be sensitive to how this is received. Considerations to take into account include:

- Who has worked with whom before?

- How long each member has been on the project?

- Who is really making decisions?

- Do the people actually have the power that they think they have?

- What were the political issues before you arrived on the project?

- What has it meant for everybody else now that you have joined the team?

- Have you got in the way of someone else's progression?

- Has staffing you meant that others weren't capable of doing the job?

There can be many informal and formal processes and procedures of which you may or may not be aware. Being an outsider you will be given a little more latitude in terms of getting things wrong now and again. You may even be able to use this to your advantage by intentionally using a different route, because it is faster and because you can get away with it. Children use this tactic successfully all of the time.

You could join a hostile environment even though it is not one of your making. This can often be the case when external project managers are brought in. Another reason for asking you to join could be so that they can blame the failure of the project on you. Sometimes clients do bring consultants in simply for this reason as it is the easiest and most diplomatic way for them to proceed. Consultants and subcontractors may not even know this is the case until it is too late.

If you are not aware of the political situation that you are entering, then you can end up in a difficult situation without having much room for manoeuvre. One of the ways in which you can avoid this is by doing as much research and networking around the project to establish what is going on. You could also be more effective in the way that you question people as you try to uncover more about a project. It is good to get an understanding of the politics and the personalities involved as early as possible. Even if this is only somebody else's opinion of the situation, it still gives you a very good starting point, and even that is better than not knowing anything at all. Never underestimate the value and insight that you can gain by talking to people at all levels of the project. Don't assume that you will not get meaningful insight from people who you deem to be at the bottom of the project organization. If you only speak to your peers, then you may not get the whole picture. Being able to build relationships at all levels can serve you well in the long term.

SUMMARY OF TOPICS

The topics considered in this chapter are outlined below.

Making changes:

- Changing the project direction, and

- Changing the project manager.

Accessing people:

- Getting to the people that deliver,

- Using centres of influence, and

- Involving stakeholders.

Improving ownership:

- Generating buy-in using pilots,

- Reporting political issues,

- Making it part of performance management,

- Working under stressful conditions, and

- Bursting the bubble.

Making Changes

CHANGING THE PROJECT DIRECTION

Once you get started on implementation, you may find that the original solution that the project was based on does not actually make sense or fulfil the original project requirements. This can be a difficult situation for a project manager, as it is then their responsibility to raise the issue and identify more suitable options. At the same time, the project manager will need to think carefully about how they will communicate the situation and what channels they should use. Whether the issue should be raised immediately or once other options have been found will depend on the state of the project and its funding. If there is a significant cost or other disadvantage in waiting to communicate then it may not be appropriate to wait to find solutions before work stops on the current programme. The following case study is based on a research programme.

CASE STUDY: PROPOSING AN ALTERNATIVE SOLUTION

On a research programme, the programme manager reviewed the various work packages under implementation. Studying the results to date in detail and discussions with the managers of the individual work packages made it clear that the research programme was heading in the wrong direction given its goals. There were clearly some areas that showed promise that were being ignored because they had not been part of the original work plans. The programme manager decided that the best way to communicate the current status and to support the actions that they believed were required would be to compile a business case for the options. In this way the programme manager could have a constructive meeting with the board regarding the issues and at same time be able to put forward the options and make progress on getting the situation resolved.

Table 7.1   Case study analysis: Proposing an alternative solution

Appropriate models	Notes
Psychological profiling	Myers-Briggs type indicator could be used to build a picture of how the work package managers' and the board's preferred ways of thinking and acting are. This will provide information on two areas: 1. Why it is that the work package managers did not raise the issues more openly? 2. How could the business case be structured to have the biggest impact on the board?
Influence	The programme manager will need to work closely with the work package managers to provide support and data for the new options. This will help to improve the capacity to influence the board into addressing the issue.
Behaviour	There could be a case of bystander apathy occurring amongst the work package managers. It would be wise to understand the root of this behaviour and to consider what could be done in the future to make the work package managers feel more empowered.
Communication	Goal directed communication techniques from NLP could be useful here in putting forward the solution to the board in a clear way.

In this example, instead of falling into the trap of group think and bystander apathy, which are the paths of least resistance, the programme manager took a risk by being honest and presenting practical solutions to the problem that had been encountered. In this way, it was acknowledged that a change of direction was necessary as soon as it was noticed to ensure that the rest of the project could proceed successfully.

Instead of taking a purely negative message to the project board, the approach of finding other possible solutions and presenting options including the pros and cons of each was proactive and pragmatic. This meant that the issues with the preferred solution were communicated clearly and possible ways forward identified. This made it easier for the project board to come to a decision quickly on how best to proceed. The project in the case study then went on to be delivered on time and was a success. And so, here the short termism attitude was avoided, by taking the short term negative impact so that the longer term objective and success could be achieved.

CHANGING THE PROJECT MANAGER

There can be tactical reasons for either keeping the same project manager in place throughout the project or for changing part way. If a significant change to the project direction and management is being sought by the project board, then it makes sense to consider changing the project manager. Changing the person involved may make it far easier to implement any changes in the project direction. In some cases, it is not possible to have the same project manager from the start to the end of a project. There can be various reasons why this would be the case. They could be:

- Going on temporary leave or training,

- Parting with the company,

- Moving on to another role, and

- Requiring a different set of skills for the next stage.

Whatever the reason for the change, the situation can be used to breathe new life into the running of the project. Benefits can include:

- Automatic review of all the processes and the project office,

- Challenge the set-up and staffing,

- Fresh view and voice to the project,

- Revised energy on the project, and

- A step change in the project direction or motivation.

Changing the project manager mid-project, however, could also lead to a number of disadvantages, for example:

- Project delays while the new person gets up to speed,

- A review of the original intentions of the project,

- Personal issues with other team members,

- Overlooking others that wanted the role, and

- Resistance against the new person.

Leaving certain team members in place throughout the project, right from inception to closure or handover to the operational team, can also be used tactically, if there are certain objectives or values associated with the project that you really want to ensure are adhered to all the way through. On short projects, it rarely makes practical sense to change any individuals as this can lead to unnecessary delays in the delivery of the project as the new team members get up to speed.

When there is a change in the person responsible for the project, often they will want to make their mark or ensure some kind of contribution that can be directly attributed to them both now and in the future, thereby creating a type of legacy. On the other hand, they may feel that they are purposefully not interested in leaving such a legacy. Each person will mould the role into something that fits their way of working and their management style.

CASE STUDY: MID-PROJECT CHANGE IN THE PROJECT MANAGER

The vision of the project at the outset was to put in place a comprehensive system for the organization to be able to provide visibility, better manage customer relationships and to drive down duplication of effort. It was also to be used to collect financial and non-financial information from across the organization.

The incumbent project manager was pulled onto another project from the middle of this current project and so a replacement project manager was arranged. They undertook a full review of the project objectives and status and decided to make significant changes to the project within a matter of weeks, including reducing staff and trimming the project objectives and deliverables. In essence it was to make the whole project more manageable with a far smaller team in place.

Table 7.2   Case study analysis: Mid-project change in the project manager

Appropriate models	Notes
Psychological profiling	It could be useful to understand the motivations of the two project managers. It looks like the first was attempting to make a significant mark on the organization by creating a system that worked for a wide range of stakeholders. The new project manager seems to be more interested in streamlining their workload rather than taking into full consideration the impact of the original project goals.
Influence	If such drastic changes have been made it could be that the new project manager has considerable influence of the various stakeholders involved or that the original stakeholders are no longer involved in the project either. This could be the reason that these changes have been possible so quickly.

Behaviour	The two project managers in the case study clearly have very different working styles. The first took a collaborative and decision-by-consensus approach whereas the second seems to be more authoritative in their management style. This could be reason that the project manager was changed by the board in the first place. Perhaps they decided that they wanted a streamlined version of the system and project team and that this would be a quick way to implement it without having to risk damaging the relationship with the first project manager.
Communication	If the new project manager has been purposefully tasked to streamline the project by the board, then it will be important to confirm that. This will ensure that appropriate support and challenge can be provided to the project manager in the future.

It would have been more difficult for the outgoing project manager to have made these changes (even if they had been aware of the need for them) and thus this replacement of the project manager enabled significant modifications and cost savings. Each project manager will run projects to suit their individual style. When a new project manager comes on board, it is not unusual to see significant changes as the management style of the new project manager comes into effect. Both Myers-Briggs and the Belbin team role models are excellent reminders that different people work in very different ways. There is no right or wrong answer. If you are a team member who is being affected by the change, then you need to be open to the fact that they may well want to do things differently. Understanding and accepting the situation by being aware of their motivations, their situation and their way of working should help you decide how to respond and work best with them.

In the actual case study, the fact that the original project champion had moved on meant that it was difficult to keep the momentum going on what was a worthwhile yet difficult project. The new project manager was not interested in being in that role and wanted to reduce the amount of personal effort required to manage the project. The anti-pattern concepts also provide a useful way in which to consider this situation. At the beginning of the project, there were far too many people that wanted to have a say in setting the scope and requirements of what the project was to deliver. This design-by-committee approach led to a system that had many benefits, but no single, strong, unifying vision. Higher level managers moved their eyes off the ball after having set a big project in motion, they then failed to continue to drive and provide direction. This project also suffered from short term behaviour, where those responsible for making decisions were soon far removed from being affected or responsible for any of the results. The longer term issues around the system's lifetime and role in the organization was not addressed.

Accessing People

GETTING TO THE PEOPLE WHO DELIVER

Projects by their very nature are initiatives that are taking place on a once-only basis. They are not part of the generally repetitive operational activity. So when an estimate is given for the work, it is based on an educated guess. To get the best planning information available, it is best to request estimates from those who will actually be responsible for delivery. Some managers make the mistake of using estimates based on how long it might take them to do the work. Unless you will deliver the task yourself, this should be avoided and only used as an indication rather than an estimate. After all, you are not the one who is going to be involved. If you think of it in terms of the seniority of staff or experience level of the staff, then you would expect better trained, more experienced or more senior people may perhaps be able to complete the task faster than a junior.

Plans are often put together at an early stage in the project by managers rather than those actually responsible for doing the task. In practice this means the plan may need to be reviewed as implementation begins by those who will perform the tasks. This often results in a more detailed plan with fine tuning of the timing and resources required. This is because the individual required to deliver will most likely have a better idea of what it will take to do the work. A manager may not have sufficient knowledge or relevant experience to make a more accurate judgement.

This is particularly the case when technical or construction projects are under consideration. Tasks will generally take as long as they need to take and it is not always possible to estimate accurately the time taken for delivery until the task is actually underway and so the schedule and resourcing will need to be updated as the task proceeds. If the exact same task has been done before then a good estimate can at least be expected.

CASE STUDY: UNDERESTIMATING TASKS

A technology research programme had scheduled a one-week work package to research options and then evaluate and document them. Normally, a solution identification and evaluation work package of this type would take several months to be completed and documented appropriately. However, the programme director saw little value in allocating the time to this phase of the work, even though the outcome of this work package would set the direction for the remainder of a costly programme.

Table 7.3   Case study analysis: Underestimating tasks

Appropriate models	Notes
Psychological profiling	The motivations for the research team requesting more time should be considered. It could be that there are many solutions that need to be carefully considered and that this would require time. It could also be that there is limited time in which to access the information that would help support the evaluation process. The motivation of the programme director should also be understood to identify why they don't see value in allocating more time. In any case, the risks and issues should be identified for having taken this approach.
Influence	The person delivering the task needs to identify ways in which they can better communicate with and influence the programme manager. It could be that the programme manager has not understood particular technical issues that would require further consideration and time allocation. On the other hand it may be that the person delivering needs to better understand the reason for such a tight deadline.
Behaviour	There could be a difference in working styles. The programme manager may only be looking for a high level understanding of the options. The research team on the other hand may feel that a more detailed study is necessary before decisions should be made.
Communication	There is a possibility of communications being misunderstood. Transactional analysis could be used to interpret the transactions between the programme manager and the research team.

A way in which the situation could be approached by the research team would be to perform a high level evaluation that would be possible in the time allocated. In addition to this, they should provide input on the further work that they feel is required on each of the options under consideration. In this way, they are presenting exactly and only what they know for sure whilst also communicating that there is more information that they have not yet taken into consideration. Providing an estimate of the additional pieces of work at the same time would make it easier for the programme manager then to reach a decision on whether they saw value in continuing with any of the options. In this way, the research team would have both successfully delivered without having compromised on the quality of the output.

USING CENTRES OF INFLUENCE

The project is under way and the team is clearly defined including all the stakeholders however, you are still having trouble gaining momentum in the roll out. Sometimes, getting additional people involved, who may not otherwise have anything directly to do with your project can be beneficial. For example, getting a board member, managing director or even a non-executive director to intervene can get your project moving again.

These people can be considered 'centres of influence' and even if they don't directly benefit from your project, they may have a wider objective, such as getting to know the other stakeholders for networking purposes or wanting to be associated with the project. They might know the importance of the project to the company and it could be in their interest to see that it is completed successfully. Engaging these individuals in a timely and tactful way can give you that leap in progress that your otherwise stagnating project may not have achieved. It is good to keep an eye out for individuals who you could call upon for support if the situation were serious enough, especially if they can add value in introducing relationships that will make the project proceed smoothly. Centres of influence can have a wide range of skills and relationships that they can bring to your aid.

Obviously, you don't want to over use them and damage your relationship or even potentially their reputation. So use them wisely and only when no other means are available. You can encourage them to get involved by, for example:

- Creating new networking opportunities,

- Allowing them to gain some experience or skill they desire,

- Associating them with a project that they wish to be linked to,

- Allowing them to demonstrate that they can make positive interventions,

- Creating an opportunity for them to return a favour to you, and

- Giving them visibility to those that they are trying to impress.

None of the reasons listed above is directly linked to the project itself. If you believe that you cannot get any help from outside your project then it can limit how successful your project might be.

INVOLVING STAKEHOLDERS

When you cannot incentivize people through traditional methods like pay, bonuses or promotions then you have to be far more creative in finding incentives that will get them to deliver for you. A useful technique for getting tasks delivered is to work some outcomes into the task that will motivate the owner. This can help the delivery along in many different ways including:

- Encouraging the owner to be proactive with you in delivering the task,

- Helping you to manage their expectations,

- Gaining their buy-in and ownership of the task, and

- Letting them become your spokesperson.

Imposing your plans and activities on others can be difficult. One of the best solutions to this is to work into the project where you can some deliverables that will add value to that owner. Perhaps adding some flexibility with the timing or the detail of the implementation will be enough to gain their buy-in. This isn't always possible but sometimes simple things like opening a communication channel or helping to raise awareness about one of their issues can help you to get the task done.

CASE STUDY: NON-TRADITIONAL INCENTIVES

On one particular project, the only way to incentivize teams to deliver the required project objectives of a software solution was to offer them some simple additional features that would make the software more useful to them. In other cases, the resistance was due to the increased workload of reporting the same information through a different system, and a way of quickly loading data from other systems, to reduce duplication of data entry, potential mistakes and resource time was found to be incentive enough to get them involved.

Table 7.4   Case study analysis: Non-traditional incentives

Appropriate models	Notes
Psychological profiling	It is not always possible to motivate people with money. Indeed, you may not be in a position to have this as an option. In which case, Maslow's theory on human motivation can be a useful model to use in identifying other ways in which you may motivate people. Employment packages often take security and safety levers into consideration by offering pensions and insurance such as travel, medical and life. Making the effort to turn these situations into mutually beneficial ones can be one of the most positive ways in which to engage others.

Influence	The ability to create win-win situations can act as a significant source of influence. This skill can be used to make progress in areas which otherwise would be impossible.
Behaviour	If creating mutually beneficial situations is a skill that you feel would greatly benefit your career then it is worth developing it through practice on live projects. You may start off with resolving small issues using this technique and then develop your application over time. This will also act to greatly enhance your networking ability.
Communication	You will need to be aware of how you communicate on this project. If you offer certain incentives to one group of stakeholders and not another then you should have a proper justification for this. Any perceived unfairness could work against you and your reputation.

The solutions that are being offered by the project manager to incentivize teams all enhance the quality of the implementation as well as create generally good process for the organization. Incentives of this kind should help speed up the uptake of the system as well as improve its longevity by having provided features that will make it more useful to the users. Communicating that there are such benefits to be realized to all stakeholders will create an open and trusting environment where people feel that they are being appropriately engaged and their wishes respected.

Improving Ownership

GENERATING BUY-IN USING PILOTS

If the success of your project is dependent on successful uptake by the end users, then it may be worthwhile getting target end users involved in the project in some way so that it helps you to focus on their needs as well as have an accepting audience for your end deliverable. One way in which you can do this is by running a pilot. Pilot projects are an excellent, low risk way of testing any new business idea. Pilots come in all shapes and sizes; from the common limited geography pilot to the limited time pilots or customer segment pilots. A successful pilot project is one in which all the issues from competition and market size to delivery and scale up are explored. The outcome of any pilot project should be a clear indication to the organization on how best to proceed.

Having a group of users whose experience could be shared is an excellent way of demonstrating the usefulness of the project's deliverables. Running pilots in series with larger scale implementations are a good way to get the right people involved with the project through all its various stages. They can also be a useful tactic to assess whether piloting will help to reduce resistance of your project's delivery. Teams often underestimate the amount of research that is required in setting up a suitable pilot that will meet the objectives. Right from the outset, you need to agree a clear scope of the pilot project. There can be many stages to a pilot project depending on the scale and complexity of the requirements. For example, when launching a product or service in a new country there will be new legal obligations that need to be understood, as well as the practical aspects of actual delivery. This phase of the pilot project should be as thorough as possible to ensure that any obvious assumptions are also double checked.

Once the scope and nature of the pilot have been determined, the next phase is to plan and identify all the necessary performance levers. This helps to keep focused. Feasibility studies, like pilots, are priceless in terms of raising many of the issues that will be faced later in a full project implementation. They can show that further research is necessary and therefore a re-work of the pilot is required. In other cases, all the important challenges that will be faced during scale up will have been highlighted.

A notable problem with expansion programmes is managing the success. If a flood of new orders appear, then does the organization have sufficient capability to manage the new business? Product and service quality standards are also often at the front line in terms of feeling the pressure of any expansion. Bringing new customers in and then not exceeding their expectations from a quality and customer service point of view can make them rapidly look for your competitors. The best way to overcome this particular issue is to think about exactly how a successful expansion would operate. This can then be the outcome that you plan to achieve.

Pilot projects often make sense, and this is true for businesses of all sizes. When there has been an opportunity to run a pilot, it has always revealed useful information and raised potential and actual implementation issues. In fact, pilots can really make sure that the practical aspects of your project delivery have been properly addressed, at least as far as a pilot will allow.

Getting end users involved as much as possible in the early stages of a project can be used tactically to try to reduce future resistance to the implementation of your project. After all, if they have been a part of your project development and implementation, then surely they would have had an opportunity right the way through to have their opinions and ideas heard on how the project should proceed. Giving them the opportunity to input into the project in this way can be a source of frustration also, as you will always have to be diplomatic about their involvement. However, in the long run if it works towards the success of your project, then it should be worth it.

The case study below considers a marketing pilot. Marketing activities can be costly and they can easily lead to absolutely no increase in sales. For this reason, such projects make excellent candidates for running limited time and cost pilots. Any kind of marketing activity can easily be designed into a small scale study with measurable targets that would define success.

CASE STUDY: MARKETING PILOT

A new equipment manufacturer had little experience on how to market the product. For this reason, the owner sought to try a number of different techniques at low cost and then decide which one worked to further invest in. The marketing manager that had been hired however demanded a large budget to throw at glamorous marketing activities without having run any pilots at all.

Table 7.5   Case study analysis: Marketing pilot

Appropriate models	Notes
Psychological profiling	The motivations of the two individuals are likely to be quite different in this case. The owner wishes to behave in a more safe and secure way with his money. The marketing manager on the other hand is new in the job and is keen to be running exciting marketing campaigns. The owner is more focused on delivering results while the marketing manager seems to be more interested in building awareness and brand.
Influence	The owner will need to sit with the marketing manager to agree the objectives of the marketing campaign so that the activities can be appropriately chosen. Since the owner wishes to carry out a low cost pilot and retain the new marketing manager's enthusiasm, he will need to use soft influence in order to gain engagement, even though the owner could easily apply hard influence in this case.
Behaviour	It could be worthwhile for the owner to try to understand the preferred working style of the marketing manager. He could then use this information to input into how best to utilize him.
Communication	It will be important for the owner to ensure that his message on running pilots is not lost on the marketing manager. Thus he should look out for wherever he does not receive complementary transactions.

The owner could approach this situation in a number of ways that would combine both of their ideas together to create a comprehensive marketing plan.

- Create a marketing plan that incorporates both of their ideas,

- Focus on trial marketing campaigns to identify the winners, and

- Focus the marketing manager on creating performance targets.

In this way, they both would get the opportunity to develop their ideas as well as following the cost constraints of the owner.

REPORTING POLITICAL ISSUES

In very large organizations, lines of accountability and organizational structures can mean that you have no ability to influence someone or to negotiate with them to help you to progress your project or some aspect of your project. In this case, if you want to get things done then you will have to elevate the issue to your management, who will then need to decide what they want to do about it. They will either have the ability to influence that team or they will know someone else who can.

There are ways in which businesses can make it easier for political problems and people problems to be raised. Using a combination of hard and soft techniques can result in good progress. Take the example of introducing into your current reporting mechanism the ability for teams or individuals to highlight such political issues as a risk or issue to the delivery of the project. And it should be managed in the same was as any other risk or issue would. Mitigating actions with appropriate owners will need to be put in place. Sometimes the owner responsible for taking the action may even be the chief executive of the company. Understanding the kind of people that you are working with, their way of working, their personality type, and their motivations can help you to come up with ideas and options on ways in which you could help them.

MAKING IT PART OF PERFORMANCE MANAGEMENT

A way of making sure that particular critical tasks are completed as required is to make them part of the performance management of an individual, the team or the department. This works best when it is part of the performance contract of an individual, as in this way the individual has a clear interest in making sure that certain tasks are delivered to meet the required criteria. When tasks are split across more than one individual, in terms of accountability, it is more difficult to get the tasks done to satisfaction as neither party feels that they completely own the task or that they will receive credit for it once complete. In which case, they will focus simply on the tasks which have been identified on their performance contracts.

CASE STUDY: IMPLEMENTING PERFORMANCE RELATED PAY

A project was having trouble motivating the team to complete tasks. So the project board decided to implement performance contracts that contained specific deliverables and targets that each individual needed to achieve. In addition, part of their pay was linked to their performance.

Table 7.6   Case study analysis: Implementing performance related pay

Appropriate models	Notes
Psychological profiling	This method of motivation may not work for each individual. So even though performance contracts have been put in place, it will be necessary to monitor their effectiveness. Further incentives may need to be developed if this process fails.
Influence	The implementation of such a process is not always possible. In this case, the project board had sufficient influence in order to put such a scheme into motion. However, this is likely to be difficult to implement on anything other than third party contracts for most projects.
Behaviour	Implementing performance targets can often result in behaviour that was not intended but that the performance contract encourages. This is due to the individual then focusing solely on meeting the targets rather than towards the full benefit of the project. You would need to monitor if there are any negative behaviours being encouraged by the new process.
Communication	The fact that the board sought to put in place performance contracts is likely to mean that they were unhappy with the way the situation was before. If incumbent people are affected by this change in process then it is likely to signal that there may have been some kind of failure on their part to have led to such an implementation. For this reason, any changes will need to be carefully considered and communicated.

Under these conditions, it would be wise for the project board to monitor the success of the implementation of performance contracts and to look out for any issues. For example, they could:

- Track performance against the contracts regularly,

- Create channels to receive feedback,

- Review and update the process regularly,

- Monitor any changes in behaviour, and

- Look out for any negative impact to the project.

WORKING UNDER STRESSFUL CONDITIONS

Keeping calm and clear is of highest priority under stressful conditions. Given the tight timescales of most projects, it is often necessary to continually review plans to ensure that all milestones are still achievable and if not, then quick decisions need to be taken on what tasks can be dropped without damaging the project. Beware of the common signs of losing control and objectiveness:

- Making project teams work late on a regular basis,

- Behaving unprofessionally or losing your temper,

- Penalizing individuals for making mistakes, and

- Making your team miss meals and sleep.

Looking at this list, you may think that no project manager would behave in this way. Unfortunately, this happens far more frequently than it should. It comes down to project managers not knowing how best to deal with deadlines and stress, which can in turn create an uncomfortable working life for others.

Having an authoritarian style may make you feel that you have things under control but you definitely won't be getting the best out of your team by behaving in this way. You will generate feelings of mistrust and people will not enjoy working with you. This will inevitably lead to people avoiding working on projects with you in the future. Certainly, good people will not wish to be treated in this way and you could end up with a team who will follow your lead. They will then never question you even if they begin to see that the project is heading towards a crisis. They will have submitted and will let events run their course. Being authoritarian means that you are taking full responsibility for the outcome even if is bad.

Simply thinking creatively about problems often leads to the best solutions and these do not have to resort to any of the methods above for implementation. For example, streamlining project activities to ensure that the highest impact activities are completed well and others are dropped ensures that resources are used appropriately leading up to deadlines. Project managers often hold back too much responsibility for themselves. It is better to delegate sensibly so that the whole team is given accountability appropriate to their ability. Not all changes that stakeholders request are possible and so sometimes it is better to work with stakeholders to come up with alternative solutions rather than pushing your team to achieve the impossible.

Project managers often shut down communication lines under times of stress. However, this is the exact time when your team will need your support and stakeholders will need reassurances. So, keep communication lines open at all times. It is the best way to know what's going on and it can give early indications of upcoming problems. Project managers have a tough job to do. But, keeping calm and in control is by far the most successful way to manage projects. So, why do it any other way?

If you are running a project unprofessionally and you justify it by saying that there is much to be done in a small amount of time, then you clearly haven't put thought into figuring out exactly what does and does not need to be done. It is likely that you are overwhelmed by the project and do not know how to focus and so make everybody work on everything that you can think of. Lack of vision will make it difficult to see when the objectives have been met. 'Must have' deliverables should be differentiated from 'nice to haves'. A successful project is when all of the 'must haves' are delivered. If some of the 'nice to haves' are also achieved then that is just an additional benefit.

BURSTING THE BUBBLE

Nobody wants to be responsible for delivering a negative message and so this can create a culture of yes men. In fact, many individuals that are successful in companies are exactly those that use this tactic, therefore consolidating the effect even further. Saying that something isn't ready yet, or is impossible is considered a sign of weakness and lack of ability to deliver. This can directly impact career progression and remuneration and so individuals are less likely, the more motivated they are to climb the corporate ladder, to communicate negative messages. Take an entire organization that has this attitude and you can end up with senior management not really having a handle on even serious problems. This is often the situation leading up to a bubble bursting. There can be lots of signals, however these will be ignored because everything is going so well and nobody wants to say or believe anything that suggests otherwise.

This is an example of group think or peer pressure. It is also caused by the fact that decision makers are not necessarily affected by the decisions that they make so that real accountability is not achieved. Some projects may be lucky to get away with this attitude without any trouble, however, this is not always the case and dishonesty can have a high price.

CASE STUDY: THE ONE CLIENT COMPANY

There are many companies that are based solely around having a single client or customer. That one client may not even be aware that this is the case and yet they are completely responsible for the success and livelihood of all of the individuals within their supplier's firm. During a recession, the client decides that they need to cut back on third party expenditure and to complete more work internally.

This decision pushes the supplier's firm into liquidation.

Table 7.7   Case study analysis: The one client company

Appropriate models	Notes
Psychological profiling	If the customer happens to be a large organization then they tend to have some level of duty of care to its suppliers, particularly, if the cessation of such a relationship would lead to major job losses and impact communities. It may be that the client is not aware of being the sole customer for the supplier.
Influence	It would be in the supplier's interest to be honest at this stage with the client about the situation and see whether they could come to some form of an agreement that would allow the company to survive. Examples of this would be offering reduced rates or discussing the option of a takeover.
Behaviour	Companies that are in the situation of having a sole customer need to be aware of all the signals that would mean that there is risk of losing that client. In addition, it would be wise for the supplier's firm to invest in seeking new customers and thereby minimize their risk.
Communication	It would be wise for the supplier to use directed communications as proposed in NLP. This would help the supplier focus on identifying what options they could propose to the client and what the benefits could be for them in coming to some form of an agreement.

Sometimes the right answer is not obvious as in this case study. The customer is of course right to reduce outsourcing as a way of controlling their own costs to minimize any negative impacts on their own firm of the downturn in the economy. On the other hand, the supplier has a duty of care to their own employees to do what they can to keep the firm operational. Under difficult circumstance such as these, it still makes sense to work on identifying options and focusing discussions on these as a way of coming to some form of a resolution. Good communication and engagement are the best route forward. Even though the outcome in the short term may be the same, there is a possibility at least then that when the economy recovers, the relationship itself will still be intact and that it may lead to business in the future.

8

Project Evaluation and Closure

Introduction

Once the implementation of a project is complete, there are often a number of tasks that remain. The outcome of the project is normally documented using an evaluation procedure. Such a document would then be used as the formal project closure report. The end of a project also normally comprises a handover of appropriate activities, perhaps to the operational team, and a release of the resources that were being used on the project and possibly their reassignment. Other activities at this stage can include:

- Sharing lessons learned,

- Capturing best practices,

- Internal knowledge management,

- Completion of project documentation,

- Payment of final invoices, and

- Ensuring all contractual obligations have been met.

This stage can be one of the most critical points in the project. Project results can often lose momentum without a good handover and support from dedicated resources to see them through. Allowing the new owners room for making any appropriate changes in the future is key to ensuring continuing success once the original project team is no longer in place. Further information about project evaluation and closure can be found in Nokes and Kelly (2007), Posner and Applegarth (2008), Lock (2007) and Reiss (2007).

SUMMARY OF TOPICS

Even at this very late stage of the project, plays for positions of power can be made and political issues can arise. For example, important information can be withheld and relevant training to incoming teams not provided. There can also be artificial reasons for extending a project longer than necessary or even cutting it short prematurely. The topics considered in this chapter are outlined below.

Managing handover:

- Creating lasting change, and

- Ensuring effective handover.

Closing the project:

- Capturing knowledge,

- Ending the project,

- Holding on to staff,

- Symbiotic relationships,

- Determining success or failure, and

- Using up budgets.

Managing Handover

CREATING LASTING CHANGE

Sometimes at the end of a project, there can be reluctance for remaining tasks to be accepted into the day-to-day operations of a business. Projects need to take into account any barriers to embedding the results into the organization. Change management and good communication often need to be a core part of the implementation plan, especially if behavioural change is a required outcome of the project. Most projects however are unable to devote the time and resources necessary to implement this properly. Project timescales can be much shorter than the timescales required to effect a behavioural or cultural change. When other parts of a project come to an end, resources are quickly reassigned and the change management part of a project can remain incomplete. Further information on change management can be found in Cameron and Green (2009), Harvard Business Essentials (2003), Newton (2007) and Herold (2008).

There are many examples where the use of hard power has been core to the solution by introducing new guidelines and processes. However, without the use of soft power like ongoing communication, engagement and training, internalization and lasting change may not occur. Hard power may achieve compliance, using influence terminology, and yet internalization is what is most often sought. The end users should believe in the new processes and understand how they add real value. If people think that they are being asked to do something without good reason, or as a way to fill their time, then they will be reluctant to participate. Internalization requires a constant and lasting visible push through all levels of the organization to get the standards into practical use. If management is not visibly behind these standards and not seen to be valuing the benefits received from such a change, then staff are less likely to make any effort to change their way of doing things.

People are comfortable with familiarity and so operational teams can be reluctant to take on the outcomes of new initiatives, particularly if this is asked of them frequently. This comes down to a fundamental desire to resist change, using Maslow's terminology. Changing the way that they do things means that they will, for a time at least, have a reduced sense of safety. As can be seen from the Maslow hierarchy, this is one of the most basic needs for human motivation. This is why implementations of the softer and intangible side of projects can be more difficult than the more tangible side, like developing and putting in the software and training people to use it.

Small businesses deal with change on an almost daily basis. If you are trying to grow a small business, then this is exactly the ability that will enable you to be successful. By its very nature, building a business requires you to find new ways of doing things, new products and services and to continually search for innovative ideas. Large businesses that manage to capture this spirit of continually trying something new and adapting is what can make the difference between survival and extinction.

CASE STUDY: RISK ASSESSMENT PROCESS

A new risk assessment process was the outcome of a project implementation. This required all off-site visits to have a risk assessment completed before the visit and then a post event risk review to be completed after the event (to capture any lessons learned and to share any best practices). However, this new process was felt to be cumbersome and staff felt that it opened them up to scrutiny and so they either failed to complete the necessary paperwork satisfactorily or significantly reduced the number of visits in order to cut down on their paperwork.

Both of these results were poor outcomes for the organization. What it had wished to achieve was in fact to provide extra protection for the individuals and the organization by having rigorous procedures that would show that they took their work seriously and they behaved professionally, thus making it less likely to have claims against them for negligence. The staff, on the other hand, only saw this work as additional bureaucracy that added little value.

Table 8.1   Case study analysis: Risk assessment process

Appropriate models	Notes
Psychological profiling	From the organization's point of view, they are trying to improve the sense of security and safety for themselves and the visitors. This reasoning needs to be explained clearly so that everybody understands the benefits of the process and the underlying reasons.
Influence	Although some level of compliance has been achieved, it is real internalization that is required for the organization and the individuals to attain all of the benefits. The organization could try putting in place performance measures for the number of visits and the quality of the paperwork. They could ensure that there was clear recognition of those that were following the process well in order to highlight the successes and to encourage others.
Behaviour	It is important to recognize that the original intents of the implementation are not being realized. It would be good to speak with the people who are required to carry out the process to better understand their behaviour and to hear their recommendations of possible changes or routes to take in order to improve the uptake of the processes.
Communication	It seems that reinforcing communication and engagement is required to maintain momentum and enthusiasm for getting people more involved with this process. This could include providing more training or open sessions where people could come along and get help and advice on the areas where they personally most needed it. It may also be useful to allocate ownership of the process to an individual who could be the contact point for any recommendations or issues on this process.

Overly bureaucratic and poorly explained processes tend to be seen as excessive paperwork and burden individuals down such that they lose sight and enthusiasm for the reason that they were doing the work in the first place. It can be that the processes that have been implemented are applied in a generic way and that they may not be fit for purpose in all cases. This could sometimes lead to the paperwork taking longer to complete than the visit itself. If many similar visits are organized then having to repeat the same cumbersome process can be quite frustrating. In the first instance the following actions could be taken:

- Interview the process implementers to understand the original intent and scope,

- Study how the process is used and if it matches the original scope and intent,

- Interview a broad selection of users to understand the issues, and

- Collect feedback from users on issues and recommendations.

The results from these activities should start to indicate the problem areas to be addressed as well as identifying potential solutions. This should then inform which of the following actions need to be taken and also the necessary content.

- Training,

- One-to-one support,

- Help desk,

- New communication and engagement plan,

- Amendments to performance measures,

- Updating of performance contracts, and

- Updating the processes to match the current requirements.

Once the activities to be completed have been identified, it will be necessary to have clearly defined objectives for each so that the focus can be on delivering the required outcomes.

ENSURING EFFECTIVE HANDOVER

During the handover of a role or entire project, a number of issues can arise. Either the outgoing party or the incoming party may not be happy about the situation and there can be difficulties in the proper sharing of information, training and equipment that can easily make handovers ineffective. It is in the project board's interest to ensure that handovers occur smoothly and effectively and yet most seem reluctant to get involved enough to influence this in any way.

There are many reasons why project handovers can be sabotaged. If you are the incumbent project team, then you want to show that you have done a good job to date and that replacing your team will have a negative impact on the project as a whole. Indeed, even to the extent that outgoing teams can actively work against the incoming team to make it difficult for them to succeed. For example, they may:

- Minimize access to information,

- Minimize access to people,

- Fail to give the necessary training,

- Fail to explain how the tools and processes work, and

- Fail to introduce the new team to key individuals.

These actions can be performed subtly so that it is not apparent that the outgoing team is being reluctant to help or even sabotaging the handover. It may not be intentional, however, even if it is not, that doesn't mean that it is any less troublesome for the incoming team. Another type of issue is when there is reluctance for the project outcomes to be accepted into the daily operations of a business. Possible reasons for this include:

- Activities considered below their ability or reputation,

- Activities too difficult ,

- Possibility of failure,

- Lack of skills or experience,

- Lack of understanding,

- Lack of personal or professional benefit, and

- Unable to get on with others involved.

If a handover is necessary, then it is important to take into account the position of both parties and whether they are truly enthusiastic about the change. The project board needs to ensure that the handover is effective and be aware of any tensions in either of the parties. If they believe that there might be any issues, then they will need to be more active during the handover period, defining exactly what they want done, and what documentation or training needs to be provided. Too often the project board will sit back and let poor handovers occur because they do not wish to get involved in the politics, even if it is their interests that are at risk.

CASE STUDY: HANDOVER FROM A POOR PERFORMING MANAGER

A project manager was failing to progress the project at the rate which the project timescales required. Despite many attempts from the project board to understand the issues, they were unable to get any clear communication from the project manager on the reasons for the lack of progress and clarity on what was being done. Due to these continuing issues the project board decided that they needed either to replace the project manager or bring in someone that they could rely on to jointly work with that project manager to make progress and communicate better.

The incumbent project manager was fearful of being replaced and as such made no effort to document any of the work done or to share any information with the new project manager. Indeed, the little that was documented was very poor quality, unprofessional and unusable. The incumbent project manager thus inadvertently enhanced the fact that they were unwilling to cooperate and further strengthened the resolve of the project board to have them replaced. The new project manager had to create a plan that was based on assuming that nothing had been done before their arrival, since they were unable to find any reports on any of the work that had been completed to date. Unfortunately, this meant that the project board may have had to authorize work to be repeated, but since there was no access to the previous work, it was more economical to proceed in this way.

Table 8.2   Case study analysis: Handover from a poor performing manager

Appropriate models	Notes
Psychological profiling	There is a clear case here of not understanding what the motivations of the incumbent project manager are that led them to behave in this way. Without this information it can be difficult for the project board to motivate the incumbent project manager either to deliver or to cooperate with the new project manager. The project board will need to make a decision as to the value that can be extracted from the incumbent project manager if they are so unwilling to cooperate and work with them. In addition, the project board will need to identify the options of actions that could be taken in order to resolve this issue.
Influence	If the incumbent project manager is not performing and yet is retained in that position, then there must be some level of influence that they are exerting somewhere in order to maintain their role on the project. It would be wise to identify the source of this influence and to work with those individuals to identify what could be done to resolve the issue.
Behaviour	Such disruptive behaviour could be tolerated for contractual reasons. It would be good to see whether there are some contractual obligations that mean that there are barriers to taking action to resolve the matter.
Communication	The incumbent project manager seems to be behaving from a child ego state. It may be necessary to use a parent ego approach in order to get the response required from this individual.

Sometimes it is necessary to work with individuals who are purposefully difficult. They may have some reason for behaving in this way, for example:

- They are no benefits to be gained from actually doing any work,

- They know that they cannot be fired or removed,

- They have influential relationships that will protect them,

- They do not wish to share any of their knowledge,

- They do not like to work with others, and

- Their personal interests are not served if they share information.

This last situation can occur when there are benefits to be had for being identified as the person who made a particular sale or successfully completed a piece of work. These are examples where the individual may receive additional payment or bonuses for a successful outcome and as such they will not wish to share this reward by having any illusion that the team was responsible for the success rather than the individual. Sales departments are particularly vulnerable to this kind of internal competition that does not necessarily serve the best interests of the company. Potential actions to resolve the situation could include:

- Changing the way incentive structures are designed,

- Replacing the individual and bringing in a fresh view point, and

- Identifying where the incumbent project manager is exerting influence.

There is no doubt that it is difficult to set up incentive structures successfully for sales departments in particular. It might be that these structures need to be regularly reviewed and tested for whether they are being taken advantage of or subverted in some way.

Closing the Project

CAPTURING KNOWLEDGE

There may not be the time or the inclination at the end of a project to complete proper documentation. Although this is a standard part of project management, documentation at the project end is rarely completed and if it is, it isn't always satisfactorily completed. It can be difficult to demonstrate that such knowledge management and documentation has value and then to motivate the project team to compile it. For this reason, it is probably the worst implemented part of any project. It is rarely taken seriously by many and a lot of the best practices and lessons learned on projects are never shared. Not everybody sees the point in wasting time with documentation for these systems, because it can be difficult to see what information will be useful in the future. There can be many reasons for this including:

- Nobody wants to be responsible for knowledge capture,

- It can quickly go out of date,

- A perception that it may never be read, and

- Wanting to withhold possibly valuable information.

Organizations can be weak on putting in place processes that capture lessons learned. It can be easier to keep experienced people on board rather than creating a system for knowledge management. This can backfire as it means that the experience will be with the people wherever they go in their working life. If you want to grow the business and make the best use of the information and knowledge that has been generated, you will need to have a system and process around knowledge management in place that people find easy to access.

CASE STUDY: INDIVIDUAL KNOWLEDGE MANAGEMENT

At the end of a project, each individual on the team was very good at collecting future time saving devices such as templates, forms, data lists, supplier lists and contact details for themselves. This information was not shared between the team members or stored on a knowledge management system. They believed it would be too much effort to sort, categorize and make accessible the information so that it was useful to others.

Table 8.3   Case study analysis: Individual knowledge management

Appropriate models	Notes
Psychological profiling	Individuals are normally good at storing information that might be useful to them in the future. This provides a certain level of safety and security against unknown events, potential time saving devices and the ability to show experience and quality of work. It is more difficult to motivate individuals to perform such tasks for an organization as the personal benefits are not as clearly defined (Maslow).
Influence	A centre of influence could be used to set standards and an example of knowledge sharing. Also it could be possible to influence people to share knowledge by putting in place appropriate recognition and reward.
Behaviour	Ownership of the knowledge management system needs to reside with someone who can help others locate information in the future. This person could also advise on how best to store the information. The Belbin model could be used to identify suitable individuals for the role.
Communication	Good communication, engagement and training will be required as well as a recognition of those who capture this value well for the firm.

There will be times when some do not wish to share their knowledge with people outside the project. This is one way in which to increase their self worth as they have captured useful experience which is not easily passed on or gained. Sometimes people don't want others to be able to reproduce what they achieved or for others to see what they have or have not done on the project. Most people are uncomfortable with giving others that kind of visibility.

Individuals like to feel that they are unique and sharing information that they have personally created can feel like a violation and impact their self esteem.

Keeping hold of unique information, your unique experience and your knowledge is something which can add value to your offering to your current or even future employer. Why then should you pass on what you have learnt to others? In any case, the experience that you have gained is personal to you. It won't necessarily have the same meaning or usefulness to others and so is it worth even sharing it? This can really impact some people's feeling of self worth and value. For the organization, documentation is all about adding value and keeping the knowledge acquired in the firm even after the individual has left.

A good example of this is poor documentation and annotation of code by developers that explains how the software works or what the architecture or design of the code is. Poor documentation increases the personal value of the developer in the company. If they write a lot of undocumented code, then it will be difficult to get others in the future to understand how it was written and how they could continue to work with it. Whether it is deliberate or not, the result is the same in that it creates problems for the company, problems that in some cases can be incredibly costly to resolve.

Introducing good knowledge management, documentation and an information sharing environment is difficult. It requires a change in culture. You cannot implement this haphazardly and expect people to see that there is value in it for them. If you are looking for people to do something that they really do not want to do, and feel that their personal value will be diminished, then how can you possibly motivate them?

Such cultural changes require change management that is ongoing, consistent and reinforcing. It needs to be implemented with the use of all the methods of influence. Using hard and soft techniques, like processes, systems and communication and engagement. You need to get people at least first to the compliance level of influence by building their awareness of such a system and then work towards getting them to internalize the change by using centres of influence and people who are good at using the various influence techniques. This could be your Chief Executive Officer (CEO), your line manager or an external celebrity. The point is that you need to approach it from all levels and make sure that people are constantly reminded that there is value to be had from making such a cultural shift.

ENDING THE PROJECT

The original reasons for starting the project may no longer exist and yet nobody takes this up and challenges the project objectives, to see whether the project should even continue. It is not always clear when a project has come to a natural end. This is certainly the case in business development projects where the progress can be quite intangible, for example, a certain face-to-face meeting has taken place or contact with a certain company has been made. Such projects can be resourced for quite some time, and without any clear objectives it can be difficult to decide when the project should end. Sometimes, the people working on the project can get really comfortable and have no motivation to stop the project as it would mean that they would be moved on to more difficult work or potentially lose their job. It can be much easier to amble along on projects where the objectives and outcomes are intangible. If you are supposed to be in charge, then you will need to keep a firm handle on resourcing and the costs of such projects.

CASE STUDY: A COMPANY WISHING TO BREAK INTO A NEW MARKET

One firm was interested in breaking into a new market in which they had no prior experience. They set up a subsidiary from which to run this project and staffed three full-time resources to develop and implement it. Those assigned to this task had no experience of this new market and were also not trained or experienced in business development, sales or marketing.

Two years later, no new customers had been received as an outcome of this initiative and it was unclear whether the project was running successfully or not because there was nothing that the project board could benchmark against. On the face of it, it didn't seem like the individuals involved were doing much and neither were there ever any tangible positive results reported back.

Table 8.4   Case study analysis: A company wishing to break into a new market

Appropriate models	Notes
Psychological profiling	The motivations of the staffed individuals need to be taken into account to understand whether there are any reasons or benefits for prolonging this project if it is clear that they are not going to be successful.
Influence	There seems to be a lack of performance measures used to monitor the progress of the project and whether it is heading in the right direction. It would be wise to get some clear milestones in place and to implement a stage-gate process that would provide a go and no-go gate to this project.

Behaviour	It could be that the individuals involved keep trying the same techniques to break into this market and therefore keep getting the same results. It would be wise to get an external party to assess their progress to date and to make suggestions as to what activities should be tried. This would then establish whether the current team had run out of ideas or whether there was a more fundamental issue that needed to be addressed.
Communication	There must be some lack of communication between the project board and the project team if the board feel that they do not fully understand where the team are and whether there are any signs of progress. This should be openly communicated to the team and the board and team should work together to agree a way forward on reporting and communication that would satisfy both parties.

Some projects seem to last forever. You'd probably look at this problem and say that good performance indicators and targets were not put in place. But even if they were, if a project is quite an intangible one, like breaking into a new market, then it can be difficult to decide when all options, opportunities and ideas have been exhausted. Knowing when to end a project is not always clear cut.

A practical way of coming to a fair solution is by tactically changing the project manager or project owner and letting them review the situation with a fresh pair of eyes and bring a new energy to the project. Sometimes, the current project team may have exhausted all of their ideas and keep repeating the same activities, whilst getting the same results. Changing the individuals may help to break any subconscious patterns that have been set up and the project can be given a new lease of life and re-evaluated as appropriate. Initial activities of the project board could include:

- Reviewing the project objectives with the team and updating if necessary,

- Communicating with the team to agree a plan and then the reporting process,

- Arranging an external resource to identify potential gaps and issues,

- Putting in place appropriate performance measures, and

- Identifying the maximum investment that can be made to this project.

This information could then be used to create a way forward in which both parties are agreed and clear.

HOLDING ON TO STAFF

A lot of business is about networking, building relationships and finding people whom you trust to get the job done. For this reason, when you come across someone in a project environment that has done a great job for you, is trustworthy and professional and you enjoy working with them, then it is only natural that you try to hold on to them for as long as possible. Perhaps, you would even try to secure them until you got started on the next project that you could move them on to. This can be a reason for the project end to be delayed. Good resources can be hard to come by and letting someone good go may mean that you won't be able to get them back as they will get reassigned.

CASE STUDY: YOU'RE STILL HERE

On one project, a single member of staff continued on in the project role for 18 months after all other project team members had left. They kept coming up with activities to stay busy with until an appropriate new project came along.

Table 8.5   Case study analysis: You're still here

Appropriate models	Notes
Psychological profiling	There is security in continuing without a change in a role with people that you have worked with for a long time. You should consider what the motivational needs of the individual and the organization are in this particular situation.
Influence	This person obviously had considerable influence in the organization to remain unstaffed for so long. Would be wise to understand the strength of their influence on others to have made this happen and bear that in mind in all communications with them.
Behaviour	If you are responsible for this person then you could use Belbin's model to understand their way of working to get the most value out of them for the time that you have them.
Communication	Clearly communicate the role of the person involved and the reason for this person continuing in order to not demotivate others.

This was by no means a unique situation in the organization in the case study. This tactic was used whenever there was a long wait between projects. The need for safety can lead to all kinds of behaviour that might otherwise be thought of as uneconomical and unprofessional. Keeping busy can be used as a career management tactic by individuals. This is also a tactic that is used by managers to keep resources tied up and 'available' until the next project is due to start. With permanent resources this kind of behaviour can be expensive for the organization. People have been kept hanging around even for years at times due to uncertainties in the organization or until a project they are waiting for gets started. In this way, when someone moves onto a new project, they can pull people that they know they work well with onto that project too. It can make them feel more confident of being able to deliver a successful project because they have members of their dream team with them. It also means that they have to spend less time getting to know someone and how they work and can get started on delivering project objectives straight away. However, sometimes the next opportunity for staffing the resource may take longer to materialize than thought before or even completely fail to materialize. All of these reasons have little to do with the project itself. They are all political issues that impact the running and delivery of the project and can be caused by:

- Resources become comfortable in their role,

- Project is comfortably ticking over,

- Individuals not ambitious and want an easy time, and

- Working in a preferred location and wish to extend that for as long as possible.

How you should react in such a situation will depend on what impact this individual has on your role or your responsibilities. If you are responsible for cost control then you will want to move this individual onto a new role as quickly as possible. However, if your task is to ensure that you get value from their involvement while they are waiting for their next assignment, then that could be more challenging. You may need to:

- Find ways to motivate them,

- Work with them to agree a plan of action and performance measures,

- Interact with management to put in place routes of intervention if required, and

- Use them as a motivational tool to embed the objectives of the project.

It might be that networking is really important for this individual while they wait for the next assignment and so you may be able to use that as a lever to arrange mutually beneficial meetings that also support project objectives.

SYMBIOTIC RELATIONSHIPS

Keeping resources hanging around without delivering meaningful work for a long time can also happen within consulting organizations, when clients hire consultants and keep them billing just to hold onto them. Sometimes the client–consultant working relationship is so successful and so strong that the client will not want to let the consultant go. The consultant helps the client to deliver their performance targets and the consultant remains desired and paid for by the client. This kind of symbiotic relationship can continue for many decades and it can also move firms when the client moves to a different firm, so that the consultant or contractor will eventually appear by their sides in their next role also. This kind of trusted adviser relationship is the core of most professional relationships and is also a way in which business networks operate in order to pull colleagues into the new organization that they are joining.

CASE STUDY: ASYMMETRIC RELATIONSHIP

A consulting assignment lasted several years with a team of consultants involved. At the end of the project, the client requested that one of consultants remain staffed on this project. During the project itself, this one consultant had worked closely with this particular client. In fact, in many cases the consultant was fulfilling the role of the client, thus leaving the client to focus on networking and finding ways to improve their own promotion opportunities and standing within the company. This worked well for the consultant as they remained staffed for a long time. This also worked well for the client as they no longer had to worry about their day-to-day activities having hired a competent consultant to complete those for them.

Unfortunately, the consultant in question felt that although this relationship was comfortable, it inherently meant that their own growth and development would be held back if they remained in this role. This is because they would no longer be available to be staffed onto other consulting projects where they would be able to gain experience on working with different clients on a different project.

Table 8.6   Case study analysis: Asymmetric relationship

Appropriate models	Notes
Psychological profiling	This is a situation where there is security and safety to be gained by both parties involved in the relationship. The client can be seen to be delivering great results whilst also creating time to develop their own career. This would in effect accelerate this client on their career path. This can also be a comfortable relationship for the consultant if they enjoy working with that client and feel that they are getting something out of it too. However, if the consultant is ambitious in their own right, then they are likely to want to move on to other projects that will enhance their value within the consulting organization within which they are employed.
Influence	There is strong influence of the client over the consultant in this situation. It will probably be necessary for the consultant's manager to intervene in a diplomatic way to resolve the situation, the likely objective being to replace that consultant with another.
Behaviour	Given the closeness of the working relationship and the reliance that the client puts on the consultant, it would be wise to find another individual that could fit well with this client; one that will complement their working style. The incoming consultant could perhaps work with the outgoing consultant during a handover period to ensure that the transition is smooth.
Communication	It will be important for the managing consultant to engage with the client effectively. This is probably best done in collaboration with the consultant on the job in order to identify the best approach.

In the example above, the consultant in question wished to come off the assignment since they had been on it for so long. They strongly felt that although it was a flattering situation to be in, it was still career limiting and that they were ambitious enough to move on. The managing consultant then worked closely with them and the client in order to make a switch or if that was not possible, then to end the assignment amicably, by explaining that it was also in the client's interest to do so.

DETERMINING SUCCESS OR FAILURE

One situation that is difficult for a project manager to accept during the implementation of their project is that for whatever reason the outcome of that project is no longer required or that the project is a failure. The original objectives of the project should always be revisited and reviewed regularly, making sure that the time and money spent on a project is still justified. There is no point in having the attitude that just because a project has been started, it must be completed no matter what. During the project, it may become apparent, as more is learned about what it will take to deliver, that it may not actually be possible within the budget or is no longer required since it has taken so long to get there. However, many project managers would feel that shutting down a project before completion is a clear sign of project failure.

Nobody wants to finish a project and look back at it and say that it was a failure or a real waste of resources. This can happen though, if the reasons for starting the project in the first place no longer exist. The project outcomes may no longer be required and yet the project may still carry on to completion, leaving the organization with some redundant process or system. In some cases, the system or processes can continue to be used far beyond their natural usefulness because people fail to properly shut down initiatives which are no longer required. This is seen in many organizations where it can be difficult to get agreement within committees on how to proceed or where the staff turnover is such that it has been difficult to keep the original objectives reviewed to ensure that the project still makes sense.

If such failures are not openly admitted and reported, then it can be difficult to get any meaningful lessons learned. No one will want to admit that a project has been a failure and that resources could have been better used elsewhere. This would undermine the efforts that they had put in. If the project board is responsible for signing off the evaluation of a project, then they will not wish to have the legacy of a failure in their career path.

CASE STUDY: REDUNDANT SYSTEMS AND PROCESSES

Reports from performance management systems, appraisal systems or customer relationship management systems are a great example of potentially redundant systems. Often they are put in place at some time in the past and their validity is not questioned and people carry on performing the tasks. Information may be collected and reports prepared in a way that are no longer useful. Sometimes, these reports have even ceased to be reviewed by senior management because they are no longer relevant or important.

Table 8.7   Case study analysis: Redundant systems and processes

Appropriate models	Notes
Psychological profiling	Many people will find it easier to continue along the same path without question, rather than evaluate their tasks and to challenge them when they don't make sense. Some may feel that there is a risk that if they are the ones to raise the challenge then they will be responsible for finding a solution and fixing the problem. Hence this would only act to increase their workload. This will also avoid the need to make any changes.

Influence	Ideally senior management should keep an eye on identifying any redundant processes as it wastes useful resources on activities that don't add value. If you are willing to take the responsibility for proposing and championing changes then it will need to be agreed with senior management. It would be best to prepare a short briefing that identifies the issues as well as proposing a solution. In this way, you are seen to be proactive rather than a troublemaker.
Behaviour	Group think can clearly lead to such an environment. It would be wise to consider whether there are any other issues that are being disguised under such group behaviour that might later cause problems. Also, if an independent thinker does come forward, then it would be reasonable to give that person recognition, reward and encouragement.
Communication	If the implementation of these processes had been expensive, it will be necessary to be diplomatic about what solutions are put forward. In addition, estimating the cost and time benefit of the alternative may be one way in which this communication could be handled.

Appraisal systems and staff grading structures can be outdated. You can come across hugely complicated pieces of process and reporting that no longer make sense and yet there is no one to challenge it or to champion changing it. A lot of resource in terms of people's time and cost to the organization can be spent in completing redundant processes.

This is based on one of the most common anti-patterns seen in organizations and that is of group think. Here nobody wants to say anything that is against the common consensus or the unspoken way of operating. It is for reasons like this that death march projects can continue. This is a common complaint that senior managers make, even though they are responsible, be that consciously or subconsciously, for group think behaviour. Project sponsors, owners, board members and senior management only want to hear that what they ask for will be done, whenever and however they need it done. They want to know that they will get the results that they require. However, sometimes it is not possible, and yet raising those concerns can make you look like you are someone who is not a pragmatic person, able to get to solutions. It only reflects badly on you.

It is only when things go wrong do people admit that they knew and yet they did not do enough to influence the outcome. Those that do try to influence outside of the group think mentality are seen as troublesome and very often seem to leave the firm or project they are working on.

In the case study, there was an individual who raised the issue and also suggested a solution. Unsurprisingly, they were then tasked with implementing the solution. Although this did increase their workload in the short term for no additional financial benefit, this situation clearly identified them as having more leadership qualities than the others. It also gave that person a chance to show management how they were competent at delivering successful projects. In this way, they inadvertently enhanced themselves to be considered for promotion and career fast tracking, having demonstrated that they were far more capable than their current role allowed for. They also demonstrated that they were a valuable resource to the company. So although there were no direct financial benefits, there were indirect ones.

USING UP BUDGETS

Small businesses by their very nature are agile in terms of the projects and activities that they run and cannot afford to spend time on activities that do not deliver the required results. They will have to cut their losses and move on to activities that deliver more benefit. Continuing on projects that are no longer required is a very dangerous use of the finite resources that small businesses have. If they carried on in this way, they would be out of business in no time. In larger businesses, this kind of activity doesn't have the same devastating effect. A larger business can absorb a lot of costs of projects that don't add value.

This can be a problem particularly if budgets have been assigned that have to be used and there are no incentives for departments to save money. Normally, this is because they would automatically receive less funding in the future. This can mean that money is spent on activity and equipment that may not be required at all. This can lead to incredible wastage that a smaller business may not survive through. The need to use up budgets can be the reason for failing projects to continue.

CASE STUDY: EQUIPMENT PURCHASE

A department was coming to the end of the budget year and they had been successful at implementing their objectives well within their budget allocation. However, if they claimed that they had been under budget then it would show that they had overestimated their requirements and that in the following budget allocation time they would naturally be given less.

To combat this potential outcome, the project manager made substantial equipment purchases in the last month of the project to use up the budget completely. In this way, they could claim that they had completed their objectives exactly on budget. The purchases included computers and other electronic equipment. They ended up with boxes of unused equipment because there clearly wasn't a need for it. It was clear to the team that the reason for the purchases was to finish the budget; however they still felt guilty as they believed that they may have acted immorally.

Table 8.8   Case study analysis: Equipment purchase

Appropriate models	Notes
Psychological profiling	The motivations of the project team are clear. The more difficult question is to identify ways of motivating teams in a way that does not encourage such wastage. It may be possible to design some incentive structure that rewards teams for being under budget and that ensures that they do not get penalized in the future.
Influence	This is not only an issue for this project, as it is likely that all projects are behaving in this way to use budgets. This could then be creating a group think environment which is not beneficial to the organization. It will be important to identify ways in which to influence the teams to behave differently.
Behaviour	Group think and bystander apathy are clearly problems in this situation. However, it is the responsibility of the budget allocation team to ensure that such activity does not occur and to find ways to monitor and guard against it.
Communication	It will be important to communicate in a way that is not accusatory as the teams are behaving within the guidelines set by the organization. Therefore, it is the guidelines that need to be reviewed and then communicated using a change management approach.

The following approaches could be attempted to find a positive way forward in this situation.

- Interview the budget allocation team to understand their recommendations,

- Interview the team to see whether they have any recommendations,

- Develop options and test these with the various stakeholders,

- Ensure that measures are put in place to track the outcome of any actions, and

- Find ways to distribute unused equipment to the benefit of the organization.

Further Reading

Bandler, R. and Grinder, J. (1989), *The Structure of Magic I: A Book About Language and Therapy* (Science and Behaviour Books).

Basu, R. (2009), *Persuasion Skills Black Book: Practical NLP Language Patterns for Getting the Response You Want* (Lean Marketing Press).

Bechet, T. (2008), *Strategic Staffing: A Comprehensive Model for Effective Workforce Planning* (Amacom).

Belbin Associates (2009), *The Belbin Guide to Succeeding at Work* (A & C Black Publishers Ltd).

Belbin, M.R. (1993), *Team Roles at Work* (Butterworth-Heinemann).

—— (2003), *Management Teams: Why They Succeed or Fail* (Butterworth-Heinemann).

Berne, E. (2001), *Transactional Analysis in Psychotherapy: The Classic Handbook to its Principles* (Souvenir Press Ltd).

Brown, W.J., McCormick, H.W., Mowbray, T.J. and Thomas, S.W. (1998), *Anti-patterns: Refactoring Software, Architecture and Projects in Crisis* (John Wiley & Sons, Inc.).

Brown, W.J., McCormick, H.W. and Thomas, S.W. (2000), *Anti-patterns in Project Management* (John Wiley & Sons, Inc.).

Cameron, E. and Green, M. (2009), *Making Sense of Change Management: A Complete Guide to the Models, Tools and Techniques of Organizational Change* (Kogan Page).

Carnegie, D. (2007), *How to Win Friends and Influence People* (Vermilion).

Chapman, C. and Ward, S. (2003), *Project Risk Management: Processes, Techniques and Insights* (John Wiley and Sons, Inc.).

Cialdini, R. (2007), *Influence: The Psychology of Persuasion* (HarperBusiness).

Cohen, A.R. and Bradford, D.L. (2004), *Influence without Authority* (John Wiley & Sons, Inc.).

Cross, A. and Hailstone, P. (2007), *The Talent Management Pocketbook* (Teacher's Pocketbooks).

Emmerichs, R.M. (2003), *An Operational Process for Workforce Planning* (RAND).

Ford, D., Gadde, L., Hakansson, H. and Snehota, I. (2003), *Managing Business Relationships* (John Wiley & Sons, Inc.).

Harvard Business Essentials (2003), *Managing Change and Transition* (Harvard Business School Press).

Herold, D. (2008), *Leading Change Management: Leadership Strategies That Really Work* (Kogan Page).

Jung, C.J. (1992), *Psychological Types* (Routledge).

Kelman, H.C. (1958), 'Compliance, Identification and Internalization: Three Processes of Attitude Change', *Journal of Conflict Resolution* 2:1, 51–60.

Kendrick, T. (2009), *Identifying and Managing Project Risk: Essential Tools for Failure-Proofing Your Project* (Amacom).

King, P.W. (2009), *Climbing Maslow's Pyramid* (Matador).

Knight, S. (2002), *NLP at Work: The Difference that Makes a Difference in Business* (Nicholas Brealey Publishing).

Kroeger, O. and Thuesen, J. (1989), *Type Talk: The 16 Personality Types* (Bantam Doubleday Dell Publishing Group).

Kummerow, J. (2004), *Worktype: Understand Your Work Personality* (Oxford Psychologists Press).

Lock, D. (2007), *Project Management* (Gower Publishing Limited).

Maslow, A.H. (1943), 'A Theory of Human Motivation', *Psychological Review* 50, 370–396.

—— (1998), *Maslow on Management* (John Wiley & Sons, Inc.).

Molden, D. (2007), *Managing with the Power of NLP: Neurolinguistic Programming, a Model for Better Management* (Prentice Hall).

Myers, I.B. and Myers, P.B. (1995), *Gifts Differing: Understanding Personality Type* (Davies-Black Publishing).

Newton, R. (2007), *Managing Change Step by Step: All You Need to Build a Plan and Make it Happen* (Prentice Hall).

Nokes, S. and Kelly, S. (2007), *The Definitive Guide to Project Management: The Fast Track to Getting the Job Done on Time and on Budget* (Financial Times, Prentice Hall).

O'Connor, J. and Seymour, J. (2003), *Introducing NLP Neuro-Linguistic Programming* (Thorsons).

Owen, J. (2009), *How to Influence: The Art of Making Things Happen* (Prentice Hall).

Peppers, D. and Rogers, M. (2008), *Rules to Break and Laws to Follow: How Your Business Can Beat the Crisis of Short-termism* (John Wiley & Sons, Inc.).

Pfeffer, J. (1993), *Managing with Power: Politics and Influence in Organizations* (Harvard Business School Press).

Posner, K. and Applegarth, M. (2008), *Project Management Pocketbook* (Management Pocketbooks).

Reiss, G. (2007), *Project Management Demystified* (Taylor & Francis).

Stanford, N. (2007), *Guide to Organisation Design: Creating High Performance And Adaptable Enterprises* (Economist Books).

Steiner, C.M. (1990), *Scripts People Live: Transactional Analysis of Life Scripts* (Grove Press).

Stewart, I. (2007), *Transactional Analysis Counselling in Action* (SAGE Publications Ltd).

Stewart, I. and Joines, V. (1987), *TA Today: A New Introduction to Transactional Analysis* (Lifespace Publishing).

Yarnell, J. (2007), *Strategic Career Management: Developing Your Talent* (Butterworth Heinemann).

Index